W9-DGW-892

GOD OF OUR UNDERSTANDING

Jewish Spirituality
and
Recovery from Addiction

GOD OF OUR UNDERSTANDING

Jewish Spirituality
and
Recovery from Addiction

RABBI SHAIS TAUB

Ktav Publishing House, Inc.
Jersey City, New Jersey

Library of Congress Cataloging-in-Publication Data

Taub, Shais.
  God of our understanding : Jewish spirituality and recovery from addiction / Shais Taub.
    p. cm.
  ISBN 978-1-60280-153-0
  1. Spiritual life–Judaism. 2. Drug addiction. 3. Alcoholism. 4. Twelve-step programs.
  5. Self-help techniques. 6. Substance abuse–Treatment. 7. Self-actualization (Psychology)
  I. Title.
  BM723.T365 2010
  296.7087'4–dc22

                        2010022251

Published by
KTAV Publishing House, Inc.
930 Newark Avenue
Jersey City, NJ 07306
bernie@ktav.com
www.ktav.com
(201) 963-9524
Fax (201) 963-0102

This is my God, and I will glorify Him;
the God of my father, and I will exalt Him.

Exodus 15:2

All praise and acknowledgment are due
to my Higher Power,
the God of my understanding
and God of my father,
Who has taken me out of Egypt—
today.

Dedicated to all those who still suffer.

CONTENTS

*Addiction destroys more lives than any other disease that is completely
treatable. The most insidious quality of addiction is that its true
nature is so widely misunderstood.*
*What exactly is the "spiritual solution" for recovery from addiction?
How does it work? And can we explain why?*
*Despite their being officially nondenominational, do the Steps make
any statements, explicit or implied, indicating certain beliefs? If so, are
these beliefs compatible with Torah?*

PART IV: HEALING EACH OTHER
The sages teach:"Make for yourself a teacher, acquire for yourself a friend, and judge every person favorably." Sponsorship, fellowship, and tolerance as keys to recovery.

PART V: RECOVERY AND THE CODEPENDENT
How friends and family of addicts are affected by addiction ... and how they, too, can recover.

PART VI: SURRENDER
Losing to win; accepting things as they are in order to change; saying you're sick in order to become well. Some of the major paradoxes of recovery.

APPENDICES

ACKNOWLEDGMENTS

A number of people were involved in moving this project from conception to fruition. This is not, I repeat not, a list of everyone who is important to me in my life – just a list of people who I remember helping me to get this particular book finished.

In no particular order:

Mark Drechsler's comments and fact checking proved invaluable. Thank you, Mark, for your help, and for teaching me the Steps so I could actually write this book in the first place.

Dr. Avraham (Richard) Leedes, Ph.D. urged me to continue writing when I thought I might stop. It is in no small part due to Dr. Leedes' positive feedback that I kept working on this project.

Nachshon Zohari, LCSW lent his clinical expertise and brilliant insight to the review of my manuscript. His suggestions were especially important in the chapter about the Stubborn and Rebellious Son.

Fr. Tom Weston, SJ helped to assure me that my writing wasn't too parochial. (No pun intended, or even desired, at all.)

Michelle Mizra, archivist at the A.A. General Service Office in New York, was extremely accommodating in answering the many research questions that came up while writing this book. Darlene Smith was instrumental in helping me secure permission to reprint the Twelve Steps. Much thanks go to them and the entire professional staff at the A.A. G.S.O. who make their services available without any cost to folks like me.

Gwen Rebbeck, editor of the *Improve Our Conscious Contact* blog, provided me with the initial forum for testing out early versions of this book.

Ernest Kurtz, a personal hero, encouraged me just by actually reading and commenting on my work. May the Creator grant him good health and many long years of peace and happiness.

To Mike Schwartz at the Intellectual Property and Permissions Department at Princeton University Press: You're aces, Mike.

More than anyone, Rabbi Yisrael Pinson, director of the Daniel B. Sobel Friendship House in West Bloomfield, MI, encouraged me to start writing my thoughts on Jewish spirituality and recovery from addiction.

Thanks to Rabbi Binyomin Bressinger, director of Project P.R.I.D.E. in Montreal, for understanding.

Rabbi Yosef Lipsker, counselor and spiritual advisor at Caron Foundation's main campus in Wernesville, PA, is one of the most amazingly positive and energetic people I know. His passion for God, our fellows and recovery were a direct inspiration for writing this book.

Thanks to Rabbi Meir Kessler, director of the Jewish Recovery Center in Boca Raton, who drew from his unique experience to help me better articulate many of the ideas expressed in this book.

Thanks to Rabbi Manis Friedman for his mentorship, wisdom and time.

Thanks to Bill H. for being in the right place at the right time.

Advance publicity for this book was one of the key motivating forces that got me to actually finish writing it. Motti Seligson of the Chabad Lubavitch Media Center was the one who first drew national attention to my work with the Jewish Recovery Fellowship back in Milwaukee and introduced me to Monique Parsons who reported on NPR's *Day to Day* that I was writing a book. "When is your book coming out?" Motti asked me after the show aired. "Hard to say," I said, "I haven't exactly started writing yet."

Thanks to the amazing team at Ktav Publishing House: Bernie Scharfstein and Adam Bengal for literally putting this whole project together, Robert Milch for his masterful (and most importantly, gentle) copyediting, and Janice Weiss of Typeworks for making sure the words in this book would look as pretty as their author thinks that they sound.

Dave from Montana. You know who you are.

To the fellows from the group back in Milwaukee, especially Jim and Phil who convinced me to start the whole thing: Thanks, guys. Keep spreading the message.

On a somber note, as this book was being prepared for publication, Ricky Leigh Mensh, host of *Recovery Radio Live*, was taken from us. The last time I spoke to Ricky, he was talking about how desperately he wished he knew more about his spiritual inheritance as a Jew. If anyone out there learns anything from this book, may it be in Ricky's merit.

And to BT.

Shais Taub
Pittsburgh, PA

INTRODUCTION

JEWS, ADDICTION, AND RECOVERY

That's Funny—You Don't Look Like an Addict

It seems to have become part of the Jewish-American cultural imperative that a rabbi has to open his remarks with the telling of a joke—usually an old and corny one, preferably based on some outdated and marginally offensive cultural stereotype. At times, this may even serve as a loose segue into a discussion of the topic at hand.

So, if I were speaking on the topic of Jewish spirituality and recovery from addiction, and I wanted to conform to standard practice, I would probably start off with this oldie.

A group of Jewish mothers are sitting on a bench on the boardwalk in Boca Raton or Miami Beach or somewhere like that, playing mahjong, I suppose, and talking about—what else?—their children. One says, "My son just graduated law school and he's been offered a position at a very prestigious firm." The other ladies all *ooh* and *ah*. Says another lady, "My son just got his M.D, and he's going to intern with the top specialist in his field." The others all voice their approval. A third lady speaks up, "My son was just ordained from rabbinical school, and he's going to be the leader of a congregation." The proud mother waits for the same spontaneous peer approval just received by her two friends, but there's nothing but an awkward silence—that is, until one of the ladies finally turns to her and says, "A rabbi? What kind of profession is that for a Jewish boy?"

My point? Would you believe that what people *think* of as Jewish and what really *is* Jewish are very often two different things?

It is fairly common to find that something that has come to be accepted as characteristically or even quintessentially Jewish is really no more than the enshrinement of some perceived cultural idiosyncrasy, as in the old Lenny Bruce routine—"Chocolate is Jewish and fudge is *goyish*. Fruit salad is Jewish. Lime Jell-O is *goyish*. Lime soda is very *goyish*." Like all stereotypes, they don't have to be true. They just have to satisfy our expectations.

To wit, there's the old perjorative Yiddish saying from the shtetl— "*Shikker iz a goy*," meaning that a drunk is a non-Jew, and by implication, Jews aren't drunks. Talk about sweeping overgeneralizations. How this stereotype even came to be, I haven't the foggiest, because alcoholism and addiction have existed since time immemorial and we find no real evidence—despite the persistence of the myth to the contrary—that the Jewish people were ever somehow magically immune from this condition. The Torah itself speaks about it. King Solomon wrote parables about it. The Talmud discusses the legal and moral ramifications of it. Even Jewish folktales are rife with passing mention—and sometimes not-so-passing mention—of the Jewish drunks who seem to have been a common if not ubiquitous fixture in every shtetl.

The Double Whammy

Now, if that little bit of cognitive dissonance weren't enough, a new, equally unrealistic, and uninformed presumption has been born in our day and age. Not only are Jews not addicts, but also, if they are (and they most certainly are not!), then, for sure, they aren't in recovery.

I mean, isn't it bad enough to be an addict, but to sit around in some room with a bunch of other addicts—talking about God? I can just imagine Lenny Bruce saying, "Being an addict is *goyish*, but being in recovery is really *goyish*." And, as I'm imagining it, it suddenly occurs to me that although it was not my conscious motivation, I'm thinking of a Jew who died of a heroin overdose in his forties.

Unfortunately, I could make a long list of Jews who have shared a similar fate. Many were even younger than forty. I could also make a long list, thank God, of Jews whose lives have been saved by a program of recovery from addiction, people who have literally returned from the brink of total physical, emotional, mental, and spiritual collapse to live happy, healthy lives of productive contentment.

There are hundreds, even thousands. And I'm just talking about the people I know.

But would either list change the popular perception? I doubt it. That's the thing about cultural stereotypes. They are inherently resistant to all evidence that would cast aspersions on their veracity. They're sort of like rationalizations but on a societal level.

The humongous irony of it all is that of all the things a nice Jewish boy or girl could turn out to be, an addict—as we shall go on to define the term in the first few chapters of this book- is actually *very* Jewish. Being in recovery—as we shall describe what that is in all of the other chapters—is *very, very* Jewish.

What This Book Is Not

This book is not an attempt to debunk every misconception that may contribute to the dangerous stigma dissuading Jewish addicts from getting help. Neither is it of interest to me, here or in any other forum, for that matter, to try to prove with facts and figures that addiction is a disease that cuts across all demographic boundaries without respect for race, religion, or economic standing. Truthfully, I find that kind of polemic to be, at last, rather unimportant and somewhat boring.

What this book is, really, is a collection of insights, observations, and even some humble suggestions based on the personal experiences of many people who have begun to relate more meaningfully to God and how that newfound consciousness and the lifestyle that accompanies it has changed their lives.

Yet, by the same token, it's not about specific addictions or the different kinds of behaviors that we use to destroy ourselves. It's about our spiritual awakening and the kind of relationship with God we have found. So, while recounting the gory details of who, what, where, and how much may provoke the morbid curiosity of the uninitiated, it would constitute a woefully boring waste of time to those who know the problem from the inside and are now living—or looking to live—in the solution.

But why all this talk about God?

Is this a rabbi's attempt to conjure up a spiritual angle on a problem that is truly the domain of medicine or psychology?

Hardly.

Recovery from addiction is an inherently spiritual topic.

Let's explain.

SPIRITUAL OR RELIGIOUS?

What Is Recovery?

For those of us who aren't so sure of the answer (and perhaps even more important, for those of us who are quite sure that we do know the answer), let us begin by asking the following question: What is recovery, and what are the Twelve Steps?

Now, for the purposes of this introduction, our answer will be brief, blunt, and overly general. This is, after all, just an introduction. Later on in the book, we will have some time to look at details and nuance, but not here and not now.

Ready for the brief, blunt, and overly general answer to our question—What is recovery, and what are the Twelve Steps?

Here it is.

The modern social phenomenon popularly known as the recovery "movement" started not so very long ago with the advent of Alcoholics Anonymous in 1935. By the end of that decade, in the fifth year of the group's formal existence, AA published what continues to this day to be its primary text—the book entitled *Alcoholics Anonymous*, which then carried the now anachronistic subtitle *The Story of How More Than One Hundred Men Have Recovered From Alcoholism*.

It was this first AA publication—today more popularly known in recovery circles as the "Big Book"—that actually gave birth to the Twelve Steps and first formally enumerated them.

The founders of AA had struck upon a way of life that enabled them to remain happily sober, and they devoted themselves to teaching others the lessons they had only learned after much grueling trial-and-error. It became clear that the program could be taught to others, but being transmitted by word-of-mouth as it was, it didn't travel very well. In an attempt to disseminate the program far and wide, a book was written. It was this book—AA's aforementioned Big Book—that took what essentially had been an oral tradition for a relatively small band of adherents and codified it as a course of clearly defined actions for others. When put into writing for the first time, there emerged twelve basic actions known as Steps, which made up the basis of the program.

The book accomplished its intended objective incredibly quickly—within a matter of ten to fifteen years, in fact—and by the 1950s, groups all over the world practiced a standardized version of the program and its Steps.

Roughly at that same juncture, something else began happening—something that had not realistically been anticipated by anybody. The same Twelve Steps that worked for alcoholics began to be adopted as a model of living by people struggling with addictions and disorders other than alcoholism. The first occurrence of a spin-off of AA took place, perhaps not so surprisingly, among the group most closely associated with alcoholics. We refer, of course, to the founding of the group Al-Anon as a program of recovery for the friends and family of alcoholics in 1951. (As for the need for friends and family to have their own program of recovery, see Part V, which is entirely devoted to addressing the subject of codependency.) Then came Narcotics Anonymous in 1953, Gamblers Anonymous in 1957, and Overeaters Anonymous in 1960. The decade in which AA sold its one-millionth copy of the Big Book—the 1970s—also saw the founding of separate Twelve-Step programs for debtors and sex addicts.

Today, there are literally dozens of various Twelve-Step groups, with millions of members worldwide, although to give exact numbers is impossible, because as a matter of policy, these self-proclaimed "Anonymous" groups keep no formal membership records.

A Spiritual Program

So we know that the Twelve Steps became wildly popular, even world-famous—at least in name, if not in content—but what is the program all about? What does it do? Or, more aptly stated, what does it say ought to be done?

This is an introduction, and we have already said we would be terse.

So, in a single word, the program is about *spirituality*.

In Chapter 1, we will speak at length about the nature of addiction and *why* exactly a spiritual solution is uniquely effective; however, suffice it to say for now that the most basic premise of the Twelve-Step programs is that spiritual consciousness attained by taking prescribed actions has a sufficiently powerful effect on the human psyche to bring about the kind of radical personality shift necessary for relieving the most acute symptoms of addiction and allowing a person, thereby, to function contentedly in sobriety.

Well, that was certainly a mouthful.

To put it simply, the Twelve Steps help people get better by teaching them how to be spiritual.

So, in summary, just so there will be no mistaking, let's recap. The Twelve Steps outline a *spiritual* approach to treating addiction; members of Twelve-Step groups are, as such, *spiritual* practitioners; the modern social phenomenon known today as "recovery" is a *spiritual* movement.

At this point, a brief disclaimer would seem to be in order. Although throughout this book and in the world at large, the word "recovery" is used synonymously with the Twelve Steps, it should be noted that not *all* recovery is spiritual. There *are* non-Twelve-Step approaches to recovering from addiction. But these are—and forgive me for sounding glib—somewhat like sugar-free candy or nondairy creamer: They exist; they may even enjoy some popularity or fill some need. But their very names classify them as a digression from the original—an alternative to the norm.

When people make a point of mentioning that a particular approach to recovery is "non-Twelve Steps," what they usually mean is nonspiritual, whereas if they talk about recovery without qualifying the word at all, what they implicitly mean is a spiritual approach.

Religion and Recovery

Now, as one could well imagine, any program for living that is so fundamentally spiritual in nature would be apt to draw a great deal of scrutiny, even misgivings, as to what its true beliefs might actually be.

Over the years, there seem to have arisen two main concerns about the program—and they happen to be mutually exclusive of each other. The program is suspected either of trying to start its own religion or of trying to repackage an old one—Christianity, to be specific. Of course, either proposition would be troubling for Jews (as well as many other people, perhaps even Christians).

Part III of this book is entirely devoted to taking a close look at the Steps to see whether they present a consistent theological stance, and if so, how we can understand this position in light of Jewish teachings about God. But once again, for the purposes of this introduction, let's not engage in an analysis of the Steps for now and just respond to the general characterization of the program as being either religious or pseudo-religious in nature.

Let's start with the facts.

It is a matter of historical record that both of the two original AA co-founders had at one time belonged to an evangelical Christian movement known as the Oxford Group and were strongly influenced by many of its basic ideas. On the other hand, it is also a fact that AA as a whole separated itself from this group before the publication of the Big Book. Another point worthy of consideration is that while the Big Book certainly uses what many would consider typically "religious" language, it never once endorses a particular faith.

In fact, it seems that the Book actually goes to great lengths—abnormally so, considering the time and place it was written, that is, America in the 1930s—to eschew favoring any particular religion or even making assumptions about the religious affiliation of its members.

For example, note this passage from the Big Book that speaks about setting aside time for daily prayer and meditation:

> If we belong to a religious denomination which requires a definite morning devotion, we attend to that also. If not members of religious bodies, we sometimes select and memorize a few set prayers which emphasize the principles we have been discussing. There are many helpful books also. Suggestions about these may be obtained from one's priest, minister, or rabbi. Be quick to see where religious people are right. Make use of what they offer. (p. 87)

The reference to consulting with "one's . . . rabbi" most certainly catches the eye, but that is not even what makes the above-quoted passage so telling. Yes, it is rather remarkable considering that these words were written when the program was not even four years old and hardly any Jews had joined the ranks of the fledgling organization. However, a far more compelling argument against sectarian classification of the Big Book is to be found in what the above-quoted lines do *not* say.

While this passage clearly conveys a favorable attitude toward (1) religious affiliation—*"if we belong to a religious denomination"*; (2) communal prayer—*"we attend that also";* and (3) religious study—*"there are many helpful books,"* it is, at the same time, abundantly clear that the institution of religion is seen as something separate from (even if complementary to) the program. It is evident that the program's authors envisioned the distinct possibility that members of their spiritual group might very well be people who would pray daily and yet *not* affiliate with any religious order.

From this reading (and many passages like it) in the Big Book, it becomes obvious that the distinction between "religion" and "spirituality" that is routinely emphasized by members of Twelve-Step groups today is not a mere construct retrofitted to the program lately (as some suspect it to be) but an underlying principle firmly rooted in the movement's original text.

By the way, do you know what that distinction is? *Religion,* say the Twelve-Steppers, *is for people who don't want to go to hell. Spirituality is for people who've been there.*

AS WE UNDERSTOOD HIM

The Necessity of Personal Experience

There's a popular phrase in recovery, which comes from the original program literature—"God of our understanding," or "God as we understood Him."

Some read the inclusion of this phrase as an act of apologetic back-peddling on the part of the movement's founders, who didn't want to come off as dogmatic. According to this theory, the extra words were thrown in to leave the God concept entirely up to interpretation and thus open to varying degrees and kinds of belief, or the lack thereof.

Others take these words to mean that God is inherently a subjective concept and as such, I suppose, no more than a philosophical construct. In other words, you can believe in whatever makes you feel good—just don't take it too seriously; it's just "*your* understanding."

I will leave it to the historians to try to prove what the AA founders really meant by this phrase and instead share with you a beautiful commentary on these words that I have heard.

Chuck C., a beloved AA sponsor and circuit-speaker of the previous generation, whose teachings about recovery are considered by many to be almost canonical, had this to say (recorded at his legendary "Pala Mesa Retreat" in 1975 and hence transcribed in the book, *A New Pair of Glasses*).

"The phrase 'as we understood Him' makes no reference to the understanding of the infinite. What it does mean is the necessity of *personal experience.*"

In other words, when we talk about the "God of our understanding," we are not really speaking of God but of our *relationship with Him*.

We do not just *believe* in some abstract way that there is a God somewhere. We *know* God, even though He is fundamentally unknowable, *because* He has touched our lives.

..... or My Father's?

After God split the sea for the Jews coming out of Egypt, Moses led the people in a song of praise in which it is stated: "This is my God, and I will glorify Him; the God of my father, and I will exalt Him" (Exodus 15:2). What is the difference between "my God" and "the God of my father"?

"The God of my *father*" (or mother, for that matter) means that which others have taught me about God. It is a relationship with God that I have been born into. I learn about it by being educated by and about the people who came before me. "*My* God" means that which I have discovered by myself. It describes my personal relationship with God based on my direct experience of His active role in my life. It is what I know about Him because of what has happened to *me*.

Both are indispensable. Both complement and complete each other.

But which does the verse mention first?

Although it would seem that the normal progression would be that one first learns about God from others and then later develops a personal relationship with Him, the opposite order is given in Moses and the Israelites' song. *First* "this is my God" and *then* "God of my father."

The basis to recovery is that we first and foremost discover this personal "God of our understanding," which is really a God of our own experience.

This does not mean, Heaven forbid, that God is a subjective notion or that He is limited to my impressions of Him. God is God; my beliefs do not change the Reality of what He is. What it means is that the Power that we can rely upon for our recovery is One who has made Himself known to us *personally*—not unlike the way in which God made Himself known to those for whom He split the sea. Recovery is a personal redemption from a personal Egypt, brought about by a personal God.

And what about the "God of my father"? Where does He come in?

I'll answer that question with a story.

Phil's Story

This is a story about Phil, the person who gave me the idea for the title of this book, without knowing it.

Phil is a Jew, seventy years young, who was brought up in America during the 1940s. His upbringing was, as in many first-generation Jewish-

American homes, "traditional" but not observant. He was sent to Hebrew school. He had a bar-mitzvah. As a little boy, his Yiddish-speaking grandfather would take him to synagogue on the Sabbath. Once he even dreamed, as a little boy, that he would someday be a rabbi. However, as he grew up, the religion of his youth became increasingly irrelevant to him. His life took various turns, and although he attained much material success, he had become emotionally, spiritually, and morally bankrupt. He was a hopeless addict. Never mind that he didn't go to shul on the High Holidays—that was the least of his problems. He was a self-confessed failure as a human being.

When I met Phil, he had already been sober for almost fifteen years. We began studying Judaism together and incorporating Jewish spiritual teachings into his understanding of the Steps. He, like almost all of the Jews in recovery I have had the good fortune to meet, was a hungry student.

One day, we were sitting together in our Tuesday-evening group of Jews in recovery. Our format was to study an insight into the weekly Torah reading as it relates to recovery and then go around the room and let each person share.

When it was Phil's turn, he spoke about "coming home," as he called it—how his life, led by a caring and powerful God, had come full circle. He spoke about how as a child he had felt that God was so very real, but that as he grew up, he had stopped looking for Him. Finally, drugs and alcohol became his Higher Power, upon which he relied to carry him through life. That lifestyle led him to misery and then to utter defeat. When he came to recovery, he had, by his own actions, forfeited every vestige of pride. And that's when he started to believe. Not all at once. Slowly at first. However, as he learned from other recovering addicts how to truly rely on God and felt the serenity that this faith brought him, he started to wonder whether he might not again see God in the way that he had abandoned as a child. What Phil said next I would never forget:

If twenty years ago, the rabbi would have spoken to me about all of *this*, I would have laughed at him. What does he know? That's all *bubbe-meises*, fairy tales. I grew out of that a long time ago. Even ten years ago or five years ago I would still have been skeptical. I had to get sober and work the Steps all these years to be ready to go back to the God I knew in my childhood. Now I pray like my grandfather did. I'm doing the mitzvahs that he used to do. And I feel him watching over me and being proud. Isn't it crazy? I had to become a drunk and an addict so I could get into recovery and find a God of my understanding before I could return to the God of my ancestors.

Recovery for Jews, or Judaism for the Recovering?

Before ending this introduction, I want to address an unspoken question that many people who pick up this book may have. Who is this book for? Jewish addicts in recovery who want to understand how the Steps fit into their Judaism? Or non-Jewish addicts looking to incorporate a Jewish perspective into their recovery?

And what if you don't fit into either category?

So here's my answer.

In a prefatory note to his book *Shame & Guilt*—one of my favorite tracts on addiction and recovery—author Ernest Kurtz explains that any insight that may be gained into the psycho-spiritual dynamics of alcoholism is inherently relevant to *all people*, for, in his bold words, "in a very real sense, *alcoholic* is but 'human being' writ large" (p. ix).

This statement has always struck me as a rather poignant way of summing up that strange caricature of the human condition that is the addict. In other words, what society may be quick to dismiss as an aberrant, irregular, or even deviant personality may, in fact, be no more than an exaggerated version of that which makes us all—for better or worse—so typically human.

And when I think of this, I can't help but also be reminded of an old Yiddish saying—*The Jews are just like everyone else, only more so.*

I will resist the temptation to make clever-sounding but absurd and ultimately dangerous comparisons that I haven't the ability or the desire to back up and just comment instead on the general idea of being what Kurtz calls, in another deft turn of phrase, "both more and less than 'merely human.'"

There's a talmudic saying, *You were preceded by the gnat,* which means that you—the person to whom the Talmud speaks—should be humbled in knowing that you are descended from those who were created on the sixth day of Creation (Adam and Eve), whereas even such a loathsome creature as the gnat was created earlier, on the fifth day.

What the Talmud seems to be saying is that it is the very quintessence of our humanness to be both more than and less than that which we were created to be. (To wit, *only a human can be inhuman.*) And while it is often difficult to distinguish between exaggeration and archetype, between parodying and epitomizing, a true study of humanity is inevitably a study in extreme paradox.

What I'm trying to say is that most people would tell you that whether the volume you now hold in your hands is a book about addiction for Jews or a book about Judaism for addicts, either way it has a highly "selective" audience (to put it nicely)—what one might call a "niche of a niche" in terms of marketing.

While I myself can't honestly figure out which of these two books I have written, in the end I don't think it matters, for what this book is really about—and I admit to being consummately biased in the matter—is the essence of our humanity, the frailty and nobility of the embodied soul and how we imperfect beings can learn to live better by letting ourselves love and be loved by a Perfect God.

If in the process I happen to dispel a few prejudices either about recovery or Jewish belief, or if I shed light on the one by describing the other, well, that is, as they say, a bonus.

PART I
THE PROBLEM

Addiction destroys more lives than any other disease that is completely treatable. The most insidious quality of addiction is that its true nature is so widely misunderstood.

CHAPTER 1
WHAT ADDICTION IS NOT

Knowing the Disease

There's an old Borsht Belt routine where a guy walks into a doctor's office complaining of a pain in his elbow.

Patient: Doc, what do I do? It hurts when I go like that (*bends his elbow*).
Doctor: Don't go like that!
Ba-dum-bump!

When it comes to responding to addiction, our first and most common response is not too different from the doctor in that corny old bit. After all of our best advice and most rational counsel have been exhausted, what else can we tell a person who still seems hell-bent on self-destruction? "Cut it out already." "Give it a rest." Or perhaps a little more emotionally, "Why *must* you do this to yourself?!"

The truth is that most people, including addicts themselves, have no idea what addiction really is. When being honest, the addict will tell you that he or she has no better an understanding of the problem than you have. Addiction confounds us; it frustrates us; it scares us. This has been the way it's been since time immemorial. That's why for millennia the only response to the town drunk was either to lock him up for good or to allow him to run raving in the streets. How else should one deal with a problem that makes no sense?

There is an old Jewish saying—"Knowing the disease is half the cure." (Yes, the rabbis have been saying that for centuries already.)

So what is the disease of addiction?

Let's examine a few popular approaches and see where they fall short of offering a complete explanation.

The Biological Model

Ask the average man or woman to define addiction and they will tell you in so many words that it is a chemical dependence. A person becomes used to relying on a substance, and their bodies crave more and more of the same until they're hooked.

That is actually a nice nonprofessional's description of the physical phenomena of *chemical tolerance and withdrawal*. It has little, however, to do with *addiction*.

If addiction were chemical dependency, then the solution for addiction would be detox. Once you can get through the drying-out period, you're home free. However, if this were the case, rehabs wouldn't have so much return business, and drunk tanks would sober-up people for life.

No, if that were what addiction really were—a mere dependency of the body—then addicts wouldn't baffle their friends and families by getting clean, starting to put their lives back in order, then tragically—inexplicably—relapsing for no apparent reason at all. No, if addiction were synonymous with physical dependence on a substance, we still wouldn't understand why the addict, even after long periods of chemical sobriety, is drawn like a moth to the flame, to be burned again. Furthermore, if addiction were really just chemical dependence, why are some people addicted to sex, gambling, and other processes that have nothing to do with introducing a foreign chemical into the body's system at all?

Chemical dependence is a physical problem, and it has a physical solution. Medical doctors can cure a patient of a chemical dependence. Heck, the deputy at the county jail can, too. If your body is dependent on a chemical, then hold tight, and get ready to feel real sick for a while until your system regains its natural equilibrium.

But addiction doesn't work like that. Addiction stays with a person— indeed, it works even harder—even when the body is no longer physically dependent on his or her drug of choice.

The Mental Health Model

Given all of the above, we may feel compelled to classify addiction as a mental health issue, an illness of the mind. If that were our conclusion, we would be getting slightly closer to a better understanding of addiction, but we'd still be left with a plethora of inexplicable facts. Most pointedly, why hasn't modern psychology developed an effective method for curing addiction or, at least, treating it into remission? Addicts have been thrown into asylums since asylums first existed. They've been given medication, electroshock, psychotherapy, and a multitude of other treatments. Yet, the typical addict will continue to confound mental health professionals with relapse after relapse despite having benefited from even the most prodigious and harrowing efforts that the field of mental health has to offer.

We should be honest in fully disclosing that there certainly are people for whom psychiatric or psychological treatment has been effective in curbing their substance abuse problem. Indeed, there are people for whom completely physical means of treatment are effective as well. But then there is that curious and peculiar lot who can't seem to keep sober for any significant period of time no matter what medications they are prescribed, no matter what kind of therapy they undergo, no matter how long they've been clean, no matter this, no matter that, no matter what. They change jobs, change cities, change spouses. They try to work more, work less; relax more, relax less; be more assertive, less assertive; more expressive, less expressive. They try anything and everything, and eventually are right back where they left off—only, in almost every case, even worse off.

The Moral Argument

Some will argue that the addict's problem is a moral one. He or she simply lacks the moral fiber or willpower to straighten up and fly right. In other words, the addict's problem is a lack of decency. The addict knows what he or she is doing and could really stop, but hasn't the decency to do so.

But is the addict, then, a sociopath? Why, then, are most addicts so full of remorse? Why do they, as a rule, suffer from self-loathing and depression?

Zealous clergy who lecture about the demon of addiction may very well have their success stories to tell about the addict who upon one day hearing a fiery sermon made a resolution to turn over a new leaf and kicked the habit, but how do we explain all of the earnestly religious folks who sit and listen to such preaching and nod their heads and yet still continue to be slaves to addiction? In what way can we understand the plight of the otherwise upright and ethical man or woman who can withstand many other kinds of temptation but when dealing with his or her drug of choice seems to lack any semblance of free will? The addict is usually aware of this paradox better than anyone and suffers a great deal of confusion and emotional torment because of it. "I'm not a bad person," the addict argues. "You've got me all wrong." But go tell this to someone who takes the high and mighty view that addiction is not a disease but a repeated series of immoral choices.

To be fair, we should say that religious types are not the only ones apt to misconstrue addiction as no more than an unconscionable lack of willpower. There is the secular willpower argument as well. Adherents of this position will tell you that most addicts eventually recover spontaneously, without any treatment at all. This proves, they argue, that an addict will quit if only he or she finally makes a decision to do so. In answer to this argument, we must concede that many people who abuse substances or compulsively engage in other dangerous behaviors will eventually kick the habit on their own. That is indisputable, and it is wonderful for those who can do so. But when we speak of addicts, we are not speaking about habitual users who can ultimately quit on their own. We're speaking about another breed entirely. We're speaking about the people who spend their lives getting clean, building up everyone's hopes, and then defying all logic as one day they jump, not fall, right off the wagon. Who are these people, and what is their problem?

Addiction is their problem. Addiction, not chemical dependence; addiction, not mental illness (although they certainly may suffer from both of these as well.)* Addiction, and not even lack of willpower; an insidious, misunderstood, mysterious syndrome called addiction.

---

* I would be deeply remissed if I did not make explicit reference to the following paragraph in the Big Book (4th ed., p. 133):

> "But this does not mean that we disregard human health measures. God has abundantly supplied this world with fine doctors, psychologists, and practitioners of various kinds. Do not hesitate to take your health problems to such persons. Most of them give freely of themselves, that their fellows may enjoy sound minds and bodies. Try to remember that though God has wrought miracles among us, we should never belittle a good doctor or psychiatrist. Their services are often indispensable in treating a newcomer and in following his case afterward."

The purpose of this book is not to minimize the physical and psychological components of addiction but to point out a third, often overlooked, element that may, in the final analysis, be the core issue that gives rise to the other aspects of addiction.

Addicts may be addicted to a substance or to a behavior. Their drug may come in a bottle, a syringe, over the Internet, or in many other forms. Nevertheless, what all addicts have in common is the incomprehensibility of their seemingly willful descent into oblivion. Over any significant amount of time, their condition gets worse, never better. They are the ones whose bizarre behavior can be just as—if not *more*—insufferable during periods of abstinence than during active use. They are the ones who are in some way easier to deal with when they are indulging in their drug of choice than when they are staying straight. They are the ones who will eventually sacrifice everything that is dear to them in order to hold on to their disease. And the tragedy is that their disease is completely treatable.

Problem or Solution

Please know that whenever we use the terms "addict" and "addiction" in this book, it is to this mysterious condition that we refer—an incurable, progressive, and most bewildering malady that defies categorization by conventional terms.

But if all of these varied misconceptions fail to define addiction, is there any way to understand what it is?

We may start to get a better idea of what addiction really is if we consider one aspect of addiction that is most always overlooked. It's something that even addicts themselves are usually unable to articulate unless it is pointed out to them, and even then it's something that's likely to be terribly misunderstood. What is this overlooked aspect of addiction? It is the fact that the addict's drug of choice is not, as we would think, his or her problem; *it's a solution.*

Yes, it sounds strange. So we'll say it again. For an addict, his or her drug of choice is not a problem but a solution. If it were their problem, they would eventually give it up. But because it is their solution—as a matter of fact, their *only* solution—they haven't any real choice of going without it.

Consider. Most people who wantonly engage in drinking, drugging, overeating, or other forms of physical pleasure are not addicts. They may overindulge; they may do so habitually, even recklessly, but they do so for a basically normal reason. They like it. It feels good. That may not sound like a very compelling reason to engage in irresponsible behavior, but it's the truth. They do it for fun. And when it stops being fun, they stop doing it.

An addict, on the other hand, does not use his or her drug of choice for pleasure. Yes, in the very beginning, the addict settles on a particular drug of choice because of the pleasurable effects that it provides, but indulging for pleasure does not set someone apart as an addict. Seeking pleasure is normal. What makes addiction "abnormal" is that the addict no longer uses his or her drug of choice for fun or recreation but from necessity. By *necessity* we do not mean chemical dependency, because, as we said, addicts will relapse even when they are completely detoxified. The addict uses his or her drug of choice because it serves a crucial, even vital function. It actually allows them to live, just as food, air, and sleep allow normal people to live. If you don't get enough sleep, you become less productive, moody, even depressed. If you don't get enough sleep long enough, your body will force you to go to sleep.

Never mind the fact that sleep is necessary for the body to function and mood-altering chemicals are not. The fact is, for reasons we shall explain very soon, that if the addict could function without his or her drug of choice, then he or she wouldn't be an addict.

That's what we mean when we say that for the addict, his or her drug of choice is not a problem but a solution—a poor solution, a destructive solution, a costly solution, but the only solution that works. That's why when you take away an addict's drug of choice, they don't get better; they get worse. You haven't helped them get rid of their problem; you've just taken away their solution. And that's why, left without a solution, the addict will always go back to his or her drug of choice. Not because they want to but because they need to.

I once heard an old-timer in AA make an interesting distinction: "For some people, drinking is a hobby. For me, it's a job. Social drinkers are amateurs. I am a professional."

Life and Death

A teacher of mine once told us a story about a group of Jews assembled at a *farbrengen*, a typically informal Chasidic gathering where stories are told, songs are sung, and there is almost always a bottle of *shnaps* to go around. At this particular *farbrengen*, which took place in Russia many decades ago, the participants had carried on late into the night. As they were about to toast each other *l'chaim*, they noticed that their bottle was empty. It was late and the stores were closed, so they went out into the street to look for someone from whom they could buy liquor. It wasn't long before they spotted a drunken peasant, bottle in hand, hobbling down the street.

"How much for that bottle?" they asked.

"What, this?" asked the drunk.

"Yes, we've run out of vodka. How much for yours?"

"Money?" the drunk cried, sounding very much offended. "No one pays Ivan to save a life!"

It was a long time ago, back in yeshiva, when I heard this story, but I've thought about it many times since then. By now, I have made three conclusions. All are just hunches. None can in any way be proven.

- Judging from his answer, the drunk was definitely not just a peasant on a bender but a real alcoholic.
- The Jews who went looking to buy the bottle late at night might themselves have been alcoholics.
- If this story really happened, it is absolutely certain that if the peasant didn't have another bottle on him, then he had one very close by.

At any rate, true or not, the story's punch line says it all. The addict is not out to have fun. The addict is trying to stay alive the only way he or she knows how, by using the only thing he or she has found that works.

Pick Your Poison

But why can't the addict live any other way?

What is the problem that the addict cannot find any other way to solve?

What condition is it that the addict is so desperately trying to treat by self-medicating with his or her drug of choice?

The condition is addiction.

That's right. Addiction.

Using does not cause addiction. Addiction is a pre-existing condition that drives a person to use. *The addict actually uses in order to relieve the symptoms of addiction.*

What are the symptoms of addiction?

They are many and varied, but they can be summed up as an overall and pretty much constant feeling of extreme discomfort and uneasiness. The addict is someone who just doesn't feel right in his or her own skin. The addict feels isolated, scared, frustrated, and hurt. These feelings are the addict's default setting. This is how an addict goes through life. Then, one day, the addict finds a "medicine" that will make those feelings go away for a while. This wonderful medicine does for the addict what nothing else can do. Once the addict has discovered the medicine, he or she can no more discontinue its use than a diabetic can go off insulin.

Dr. William D. Silkworth, the specialist who treated AA co-founder Bill Wilson in the hospital noted what he considered the common characteristic of those alcoholics who were untreatable by medical means:

> To them, their alcoholic life seems the only normal one. They are restless, irritable and discontented, unless they can again experience the sense of ease and comfort which comes at once by taking a few drinks . . . (*Alcoholics Anonymous*, pp. xxviii–xxix)

Of course, Silkworth had no idea what made this so; all he knew was that (a) alcoholics generally feel miserable all the time, and (b) they briefly experience almost total relief by becoming intoxicated. This double-bind makes someone an addict.

As a longtime member of OA (Overeaters Anonymous) once told me, "I don't qualify for OA membership because of all the problems that food caused me. I qualify for OA because of all the problems I fixed with food."

Of course, you can't really fix a problem with food or with booze or with drugs or with gambling or with sex. However, for the addict, the momentary relief from existential suffering is the closest he or she can get and is a great enough payoff to justify any and every expense. As the Satan remarked in the Book of Job (2:4): "Only skin for skin, but a person will give everything for his life."

What was the Adversary saying? A person will only give up some skin, something superficial, to save skin, some other extraneous thing. For instance, if you are falling, you might put your hands out to break your fall and scrape the skin on your hands in order not to scrape the skin on your face. But you wouldn't risk your life in order to avoid getting a scrape on your face. That's what it means, "Only skin for skin."

That's why a nonaddict with a substance abuse problem will stop using when the consequences become too costly. A nonaddict might be willing to make certain sacrifices for the sake of having a good time but will not want to play for keeps. An addict, on the other hand, will not stop no matter what the stakes, for a person will willingly risk any sacrifice in order to live.

Of course, the irony is that the addict's drug of choice is actually causing death. But for the addict, it doesn't seem so. It seems the opposite. We mentioned this point earlier and said that it would be explained, so here is an explanation.

Consider the following analogy. A person, God forbid, is suffering from an incurable disease of the body. The doctors say that they cannot make it go away but they may be able to force it into remission with chemotherapy. Now, the doctors admit that the chemotherapy has dangerous side-effects; it may even kill the patient before the disease does, but if they do nothing, the disease will surely be fatal. That is precisely the dilemma that the addict faces in using or not using his or her drug of choice.

CHAPTER 2
WHAT ADDICTION ACTUALLY IS

Causes and Symptoms

Now that we understand that for an addict, using is actually his or her best attempt at treating the real problem, we must ask: *What is that real problem?* In so many words, we have already said that the addict has a fundamental inability to live peacefully and contentedly and uses his or her drug of choice to induce a temporary state of relief from his or her deep, incessant discomfort with life.

But that still doesn't really answer the question. It still doesn't tell us what the problem really is. *What is it that makes the addict unable to handle life in the first place?* If we were speaking of a physical malady, say, congestive heart failure, we wouldn't say that the person's problem is a pain in the chest. The pain is a symptom. The problem is that the coronary artery is clogged shut. So, too, the fact that addicts are miserable when not using is a symptom of the problem. Addicts already know well and good how to treat the symptoms: they use. The only way an addict can ever have a real choice to stop self-medicating the symptoms is if he or she can understand and treat the real problem that gives rise to the symptoms to begin with.

The Spiritual Model

This is the story of an alcoholic whose story indirectly came to change the lives of millions of alcoholics and addicts around the world. His story is not well known, not even among those whose recovery they have to thank him for.

Rowland Hazard was born in 1881 to a rich and powerful family of Rhode Island mill owners. He graduated from Yale in 1903, served in the Rhode Island state senate, and ran a number of businesses. All that time, he drank compulsively while his family tried to hide the problem. He had been to one sanitarium after another but to no avail. Rowland would go on long drinking sprees that would often take him to exotic locales all around the world. At some point, in the early 1930s, Rowland found himself in Zurich, Switzerland, receiving the very best help that money could buy under the care of the world-renowned psychiatrist Dr. Carl Jung.

With Jung's counseling, Rowland finally thought he had his problem licked. After his release, however, he immediately relapsed and returned to the doctor a broken man. Jung told Rowland that his condition was hopeless and that he had never seen an alcoholic of his type recover. At that moment, Rowland was profoundly shaken. He asked the doctor whether there were ever any exceptions. Jung responded that for an alcoholic of the type he was, instances of recovery were so rare as to be considered an anomaly. However, whenever such isolated cases had occurred, they had something in common. Jung then referred to what he called "a vital spiritual experience." Though he admitted that he did not exactly understand how it worked, he knew that the "vital spiritual experience" was sufficiently powerful to effect no less than a complete "psychic change" in the individuals who had them. Jung said that he had actually been trying therapeutically to induce the onset of such an experience in Rowland but had been unsuccessful.

Said the doctor:

> To me these occurrences are phenomena. They appear to be in the nature of huge emotional displacements and rearrangements. Ideas, emotions, and attitudes which were once the guiding forces of the lives of these men are suddenly cast to one side, and a completely new set of conceptions and motives begin to dominate them. (*Alcoholics Anonymous*, p. 27)

Rowland was encouraged by the knowledge that his problem might have a solution, even one as unusual as the doctor had described, but he was puzzled. He was already a religious man and asked why that had not already led to the solution that the doctor described. Jung explained that mere religious affiliation had nothing to do with what he meant. Rowland was in need of a vital spiritual experience, not ceremony and doctrine, but an actual encounter with the Divine. Jung suggested that Rowland immerse himself in a spiritual environment, earnestly seek a higher consciousness, and pray that something would happen.

Armed with this information, Rowland set out to effect a radical spiritual change within himself. He found eventual success toward this end by joining the Oxford Group, a popular religious movement of the day that stressed rigorously honest self-reflection, prayer, and meditation.

The story continues. In 1934, Ebby Thacher, son of a prominent New York family, was about to be locked up because of his alcoholism. The presiding judge in the case had a son who was a member of the same Oxford Group and a friend of Rowland. The judge's son, along with Rowland and another Oxford Group member, convinced the judge to release Ebby to their care, whereupon they prevailed upon him to seek a spiritual solution to his drinking problem as Rowland had done. Ebby pursued their path and found the results to be astonishingly effective.

This same Ebby was a childhood friend of a man named Bill Wilson who was also a chronic drunk. Bill was out of work, depressed, and in dangerously bad health. One day, Ebby appeared in Bill's Brooklyn home and transmitted to him the spiritual principles upon which he was managing to stay happily sober. Bill was put off by what he perceived to be his friend's religious zeal, but Ebby assured him that he was not seeking to convert him. Ebby told Bill that theology and dogma were not necessary. All he needed to do in order to begin was to be willing to have a relationship with God and to live according to some basic spiritual principles. What's more, all this could be done regardless of whatever conception of God he had.

The basic ideas that Ebby conveyed to Bill, as Bill would later recall, were simple. Here they are as transcribed from one of Bill's public AA talks:

We admitted we were licked.

We got honest with ourselves.

We talked it over with another person.

We made amends to those we had harmed.

We tried to carry this message to others with no thought of reward.

We prayed to whatever God we thought there was.

These simple and elementary concepts were not religious but spiritual. The difference was not lost on Bill.

Ebby's visit planted a seed in Bill that would soon sprout into a vital spiritual experience of Bill's own. For Bill, the experience was dramatic and sudden but its results seemed to be long lasting. For the first time in his life, Bill was staying sober. Months later, he would meet Dr. Bob Smith, an alcoholic physician from Akron, Ohio, and transmit to him the message that he had learned from Ebby, that Ebby got from Rowland and the Oxford Group and that Rowland received from Carl Jung.

Through the collaboration of Wilson and Smith, these principles would develop into the program called Alcoholics Anonymous, the essence of which is summed up in the program's Twelve Steps. In the ensuing decades, these same Steps would be applied to recovery from other addictions and work just as effectively.

For the first time in history, there was a successful treatment for the disease of addiction—a treatment that was neither physical nor psychological nor even religious but *spiritual*. By living according to basic *spiritual* principles, addicts were not just able to remain abstinent but also to lead happy and productive lives while doing so.

The Real Problem

Now we are in a better position to answer the question we asked earlier. What is the real problem the addict is attempting to treat by using? The real problem, as we can now understand, is a spiritual problem, as evidenced by the fact that the real solution is a spiritual solution.

Let us now ask, what is the exact nature of the spiritual problem? What does it mean to be spiritually sick? In other words, what is the root cause of the spiritual illness called addiction?

Let's continue with the story.

In 1961, decades after Bill was first introduced to Jung's spiritual approach to treating alcoholism and AA had already bloomed into a massive movement all over the world, Bill wrote Jung a long-overdue letter of thanks. In the letter, he marvels at how Jung had managed to ascertain that the only real treatment for alcoholism was a spiritual one, especially since it was such a radical stance at the time.

In his response, Jung begins by admitting that he had to overcome his own reluctance to offer such counsel because it was indeed considered unconventional at the time. He then goes on to recall his impressions of his former patient, Rowland, and of alcoholism in general:

> [The patient's] craving for alcohol was the equivalent, on a low level, of the spiritual thirst of our being for wholeness, expressed in medieval language: the union with God. How could one formulate such an insight in a language that is not misunderstood in our days? (Letter to Wilson, 1961)

These are heavy concepts—"the spiritual thirst of our being for wholeness," "union with God." It's understandable how it might seem presumptuous to use such terms when describing a condition that most people see as no more than a chemical dependency, a mental disorder, or a lack of will. But history would bear testimony to the fact that Jung's understanding of the problem, and its solution as later applied by Wilson, were astoundingly accurate.

Sick for God

So now we have our answer. The addict is sick with a yearning for God and can only become well by having some contact with God.

It sounds grandiose, I know. What are we saying? That all addicts are really supersensitive, spiritually passionate seekers?

Not exactly.

More aptly stated: *All* human beings have a deep-seated need for spiritual contact. But most people can also live their lives without it. Addicts are people who, for whatever reason, are unsettled to the core and cannot handle the business of life without maintaining a continual and acute awareness of the Divine. Absent such higher consciousness, they are miserable and sick. What makes their dilemma fatal is that their drug of choice will actually produce in them short-term effects that *simulate* the release and relief that can only *really* be had through spiritual consciousness. Consequently, the only real treatment for their condition is to make sure that they get the "real thing" instead of self-medicating with the fake stuff, for if they do not get the real thing, they *have no choice* but to take the fake stuff.

In other words, for most people, spirituality is a luxury, something to be sought after more "basic" needs are met. Addicts are somehow different

PROF. DR. C. G. JUNG

KÜSNACHT-ZÜRICH
SEESTRASSE 228

January 30, 1961

Mr. William G. Wilson
Alcoholics Anonymous
Box 459 Grand Central Station
New York 17, N.Y.

Dear Mr. Wilson,

your letter has been very welcome indeed.

I had no news from Roland H. anymore and often wondered what has been his fate. Our conversation which he has adequately reported to you had an aspect of which he did not know. The reason was, that I could not tell him everything, was that those days I had to be exceedingly careful of what I said. I had found out that I was misunderstood in every possible way. Thus I was very careful when I talked to Roland H. But what I really thought about, was the result of many experiences with men of his kind.

His craving for alcohol was the equivalent on a low level of the spiritual thirst of our being for wholeness, expressed in mediaeval language: the union with God.¹⁾

How could one formulate such an insight in a language that is not misunderstood in our days?

The only right and legitimate way to such an experience is, that it happens to you in reality and it can only happen to you when you walk on a path, which leads you to higher understanding. You might be led to that goal by an act of grace or through a personal and honest contact with friends, or through a higher education of the mind beyond the confines of mere rationalism. I see from your letter that Roland H. has chosen the second way, which was, under the circumstances, obviously the best one.

I am strongly convinced that the evil principle prevailing in this world, leads the unrecognized spiritual need into perdition, if it is not counteracted either by a real religious insight or by the protective wall of human community. An ordinary man, not protected by an action from above and isolated in society cannot resist the power of evil, which is called very aptly the Devil. But the use of such words arouse so many mistakes that one can only keep aloof from them as much as possible.

These are the reasons why I could not give a full and sufficient explanation to Roland H. but I am risking it with you, because I conclude from your very decent and honest letter, that you have acquired a point of view above the misleading platitudes, one usually hears about alcoholism.

You see, Alcohol in Latin is "spiritus" and you use the same word for the highest religious experience as well as for the most depraving poison. The helpful formula therefore is: spiritus contra spiritum.

Thanking you again for your kind letter

I remain

yours sincerely

C. G. Jung.

¹⁾ "As the hart panteth after the water brooks, so panteth my soul after thee, O God." (Psalm 42,1)

Facsimile of Dr. C.G. Jung's letter to AA Co-founder, Bill Wilson.

in this respect in that for them, there can be nothing resembling a normal life if their spiritual needs are not met first.

Of course, we don't mean to say that only addicts are capable of truly yearning for God. In Song of Songs (2:5), King Solomon describes the feeling of being "lovesick" for God. That is not the point anyway. It is not the longing for spiritual wholeness that causes addiction. What makes an addict an addict is the *combination* of *two* factors: (1) they are profoundly disturbed and unsettled with their own existence as an entity apart from God; and (2) for reasons unknown, they can somehow briefly simulate relief from this condition by taking their drug of choice.

This is the trap of addiction, and it is the real problem we have been trying to define. The real problem that lies at the core of addiction is that addicts are people who are in dire need of a relationship with God but are able to substitute fulfilling this need with a behavior that is essentially self-destructive.

Really, the drug of choice becomes the addict's God. This is not meant as mere rhetoric. Addiction is idol worship in the most fundamental sense of the term—turning to something other than God to do for you what only God can do.

The Double Header

I once had a double speaking engagement at a synagogue that also hosted a Jewish recovery program. From seven to eight, I was the speaker at the regular synagogue function, and then I walked to the other side of the building and spoke to the addicts from eight until nine.

I spoke to the first group about some basic ideas of Jewish spirituality and how they apply to living a better life. After speaking to that group, I felt like a sales clerk whose client indulges him to give a long, elaborate pitch for an item that they both know the client isn't going to buy. Maybe it was me. Maybe I was off that night. Whatever the reason, I felt that most of the crowd really had no use for the ideas that I was trying to communicate.

I headed down the hall to the other group and prepared myself to deliver what was essentially the same lecture that I had just given, only with some recovery language thrown in. When I got to the room full of addicts, I was suddenly struck with a wonderful feeling. I probably get this same vibe every time I speak to addicts, but this time, the contrast, having just spoken to another group minutes earlier, was immediate. These people weren't interested in seeing me put on a show. They were there to hear me as if their very lives depended on it. Mind you, they were not tense or melancholic. They were enjoying themselves. Nevertheless, at the same time, there was a collective sense of urgency.

As I started talking, I found myself speaking about what Jung described as "the spiritual thirst of our being for wholeness . . . the union with God."

"Why do we yearn to be at one with God?" I asked. "What is it about us that makes us feel uncomfortable as an entity apart from God?"

I proceeded to explain what chasidus (the mystical teachings of the Chasidic masters) says about the very nature of separate consciousness being a painful delusion, an error in thinking that must be rejected in favor of the absolute truth that we do not really have an existence that is independent from the all-encompassing, all-pervasive Unity of All.

I cannot claim that these were my exact words verbatim, but it went pretty much like this:

When God created the world, what were His raw materials? What did He start with? The answer, of course, is nothing. The world came into being at some point, but before that, it was nothing. God was always Something even before He created the world and will always be Something with or without a world, but the world and everything in it was once nothing.

There's a joke about a team of scientists who, studying the Book of Genesis, decide they can replicate the creation of man just as it was done the first time by God. They gather up a pile of dirt and hook it up to a big machine by electrodes. The leader of the team opens his Bible and reads, "The Lord God formed the man from the dust of the ground and breathed into his nostrils the breath of life." As they are about to throw the switch and animate this lump of earth into a living, breathing man, a voice booms out from Heaven, "Hey! Get your own dirt!"

Human creativity is not real creation. As humans, we can change one something into another something. Whether we speak of the artist who turns paint and canvas into a masterpiece or a builder who turns steel and glass into a skyscraper, we are talking about the manipulation of form, not the creation of new existence. Indeed, the First Law of Thermodynamics is that matter and energy cannot be created or destroyed; they can only be changed into different forms.

Yet, if we believe that the universe has a beginning, we must say that God started by taking nothing and making it into something. In so doing, God did not just change the form of nothing. He overrode its very essence. The very definition of nothing is that it does not exist. By forcing nothing to be something, God made nothing be the very opposite of what it really is.

Now, when we form one something into another, it usually keeps the shape we put it in. A loaf of bread isn't going to disassemble itself back into flour and water. A plastic cup isn't going to revert to petroleum. Why? Because for flour and water to be bread and for petroleum to be a plastic cup is no imposition at all upon the essence of flour and water or petroleum. Their essence hasn't changed, only their form.

When God turned nothing into something, He completely changed its essence. Every moment that nothing exists as a something is unnatural. Indeed, nothing would not even continue to be something unless it's constantly being *forced* to do so, which is why we say that creation is necessarily an on-going process.

At any rate, if you exist, then you are a something. But that's only because God is creating you that way at this instant. Your essence is to be nothing. Or, should we say, your true and natural state is to have no existence of your own and to exist only as He exists, within the totality and oneness of God.

If that's the case, then it explains the mystery of why it can be painful just to exist.

Our somethingness is not our true essence. Oneness is our true essence. Not that it bothers all of us equally. Some people can live with it. Some people can't. But the people who can live with it are sitting down the hall in the other room while the people who can't are sitting right here!

CHAPTER 3
SELF-CONSCIOUSNESS AND GOD-CONSCIOUSNESS

Self-Obsession

It should make sense now when we say that one way of describing the problem of addiction is to say that the addict is simply way too in tune with his or her own existence. Addicts are often described as being touchy or hypersensitive. It's true. Hence, the insatiable urge to numb themselves into unconsciousness. Long gone are the days when they were actually enjoying their use. They are actually looking for the self-obliteration their use brings on.

I once heard an addict relate how when he first got sober, people told him that if he just didn't drink or use, he would feel better. "Yeah, when you get sober, you feel better, alright. You feel anger better; you feel resentment better; you feel fear better."

What the process of recovery does, in essence, is to allow the addict to find self-*transcendence* instead of self-*destruction*. The immediate effects of self-transcendence and self-destruction can feel quite similar. The difference is that with self-destruction, beside the fact that one drives oneself to a miserable death, it doesn't really address the root problem. A person who is focused on blotting out his or her own self is still focused on self. The only solution is to start to rise above the self, to transcend it. This is the essence of spirituality and having a conscious relationship with God.

Those who are still uncomfortable with the whole idea of God might jump to theorize that the addict could gain the same relief by focusing on anything outside of the self. The problem is that this just doesn't work. Human beings just aren't wired that way, especially addicts.

I'll tell you the story of how we got that way. It's actually the story of addiction and recovery in macrocosm, as related by the Zohar, the canonical text of Kabbalah.

In the Garden

Before the sin of the Tree of Knowledge, Adam and Eve had no self-concept. It simply wasn't built into the human psyche to be self-aware. Human consciousness was nothing like we know it today. Adam and Eve saw themselves, and all of creation, as one great unity at one with God and they had no other concept of existence. Indeed, that's why the voice of temptation came to them through the Serpent and not from their own minds as it comes to us. They were simply incapable of even conceiving the very notion that one might have any other function or goal than being in total harmony with God.

That is why Adam and Eve in the garden were able to be naked and not be ashamed. They understood that they had no clothes on. But it didn't mean anything to them. What reason is there to be ashamed of having the parts that God gave you? Indeed, the whole concept of shame was unknown to them.

When they ate of the Tree of Knowledge, however, "their eyes were opened" (Genesis 3:7). The knowledge that they gained was self-knowledge, the awareness of their own existence as something separate from God. In very practical terms, this means that they realized that their bodies and senses could be used purposely to *obtain* pleasure rather than just experiencing whatever was happening in the moment. To be sure, even before the sin, Adam and Eve felt pleasure, but it was a sensation of "this is pleasure," rather than "I feel good." With "I feel good" comes "I feel bad." And with that comes "You know what would make me feel good?" and "I am afraid that that will make me feel bad." All at once, they suddenly experienced the capacity to *feel what they were feeling*. This is not to be confused with the capacity to feel. They had that before. What they experienced for the first time were all of the *feelings of feeling*, which are not really feelings at all but a subjective interpretation of objective experience. No longer could they just "be." They were forced to be aware of their own reaction to stimulus.

Noah's Vineyard

As descendants of that first man and woman, we have inherited their hard-wiring. It is inextricable from the human condition that we feel awareness of self. This self-consciousness is impossible to overcome on our own. It comes from feeling separate from God and can only be relieved by feeling at one with Him again. The oneness with God that Adam and Eve felt before the sin was automatic. The oneness of God that we experience must be the result of a conscious decision.

Early in human history, there was a great man who tried to reverse the effects of the Sin of the Tree of Knowledge. His name was Noah. After the Flood, he observed a new world and thought it the perfect time to introduce a new paradigm of human existence. If humanity's fatal flaw was self-consciousness, it could be remedied, he thought, by destroying consciousness. Immediately after disembarking from the Ark, "Noah . . . planted a vineyard. He drank its wine and got drunk" (Genesis 9:20–21).

The shameful results of Noah's foray into wiping out his own consciousness were immediate. When Noah came to, he found that not only had he not been elevated but also that he was degraded and abused.

Our Mother Sarah

Says the Zohar, after the failures of Eve and Noah, the matriarch Sarah discovered the real solution to humanity's problem. The Kabbalah explains that Sarah was the personification of humility and selflessness. Many stories illustrate Sarah's selfless nature, for this was not only a motif in her life but also an expression of her very essence.

For instance, when Sarah and her husband, Abraham, briefly visited Egypt looking for food, Sarah had to be smuggled into the country while hiding in a box. This was for her own safety, as we see later, for when she was eventually discovered, she was abducted and taken to the palace of the king. However, the very fact that she was willing to go along with the plan is remarkable.

Furthermore, during that same journey, she agreed with Abraham to tell people that she was his sister rather than his wife—she was indeed his kinswoman, his niece to be precise—so that no one would kill Abraham in order to be able to lawfully marry his wife. (In those days, people would commit murder sooner than they would go after a married woman.) Again, this was for practical considerations, but her willingness to refrain from revealing her identity is extraordinary.

Many years later, when Sarah and Abraham were older and still had not had children, Sarah told Abraham to take a concubine and have a child with her. (Although this was a common and accepted practice in those days, it was still unusual that a wife would actually encourage her husband to do so.)

Modern sensibilities recoil from these stories. "She was an oppressed woman!" people today will cry. "How awful for her!" they will say. If modern sensibilities had garnered us one iota of the happiness that Sarah had in life, these objections might be worth listening to.

Sarah was not a weak woman. She was a strong woman. She was not timid. She was brave. And most of all, she was happy. She was happy because she had discovered the secret of living selflessly. Our mother Sarah is our role model for the power, the joy, and the freedom of the selfless life.

At the age of ninety, Sarah finally had a son and she named him Isaac, which means "laughter." Yes, Sarah named the child, not Abraham, for she was infused with a greater prophetic spirit than her husband. Prophecy is the condition of being a completely open and unobstructed conduit of the Divine. This was Sarah's essence.

Now, Abraham's concubine had given birth to a son years earlier. His name was Ishmael. When Ishmael came of age and Sarah saw that he had become a physical and spiritual danger to her son, Isaac, she ordered her husband to banish Ishmael from their home. (Sarah was definitely not a codependent, but we shall speak at length on that subject in later chapters.)

Again, modern sensibilities see this last episode as incongruous with Sarah's mild, easy-going nature. What modern sensibilities fail to grasp is that for Sarah, ordering her husband to send away his other son was not a sudden departure from her selfless nature. It was the ultimate expression of it. Sarah had no problem setting boundaries. She had no hesitation to speak the truth. Because there was not one bit of self-consciousness involved in her assessment of the situation.

And do you know what God told Abraham when he was unenthusiastic about following her advice? "All that Sarah tells you, listen to her voice" (Genesis 21:12). And as the Midrash elucidates, "For she is greater in prophecy than you."

Sarah was happy, and her example teaches all of us how to be happy. Sarah perfected the skill of self-detachment, of rising above the conscious ego. Sarah never had to second-guess herself when making a difficult decision because her self was never part of the decision to begin with.

If only we could all be like Sarah—God-conscious rather than self-conscious; self-transcendent rather than self-indulgent or self-destructive.

But how?

Let's discuss the problem a bit more so that we may clearly understand how to truly break free of it.

Another Name for Self

A teacher of mine once told us a parable about the Angel of Death complaining to God that his name was bad for business.

The Angel of Death stands before the Heavenly Throne and says:

"Master, You have appointed me with the task of making it necessary for the humans to actually exercise their free choice if they wish to be close to You. I am trying to do my job and make them feel that there are options other than having a relationship with You. But they do not listen, and I think it is the name You have given me. Whenever I introduce myself to humans, they hear the word 'death' in my name and run away in terror. If I am to continue doing my job, I must be called something else."

"Very well," said God. "You may call yourself Satan, the Adversary. Go to the humans and do as you have been ordered."

The Angel of Death/Adversary did so, but was back a little while later.

"This name is no good either," he said. "Once people know that I am the Adversary, they know that I don't have their best interests at heart. They don't trust me."

"So call yourself the Evil Inclination," God said. "That sounds a little more innocuous."

So the Angel of Death/Adversary/Evil Inclination went to try out his new name, but it wasn't long before he was back protesting that this name, too, was no good.

"It has the word 'evil' right there in the name. That's showing all of my cards! I need a name that won't scare people off."

"Try Animal Soul," suggested God.

And so he did. But he found that it didn't completely work either.

"People don't listen to animals. I get no respect with this name."

"All right," said God, "I didn't want to have to do this, but I have a name for you that will allow you to do all of your business without any problem at all. You'll be able to confuse and mislead them as much as you need to and they will insist to themselves that what you are saying makes sense. They will not want to make a decision without first consulting you. They will believe that you are helping them, and they will actually feel silly and embarrassed when they doubt your advice. It's really such a perfect name for what you do. Go and tell them that your name is Self."

And so he did. And since then, there's been so much business that Self has had to hire a different assistant to deal with each one of us.

E.G.O.

The recovery culture is full of hundreds of pithy and original sayings, many of which you will find sprinkled throughout this book. Especially popular are "backronyms," made-up acronyms that are retrofitted for real words. Addicts say they can be thickheaded so they like aphorisms that are easy to remember. One such reverse acronym is E.G.O., which stands for "Edging God Out."

One cannot be at once God-conscious as well as self-conscious. It's not that the ego is inherently evil; it's just the *source* of evil. The ego says, "I exist. God is bigger, stronger, and older than I am, but I also exist."

Of course, that doesn't sound so terribly sinister, but that's precisely what makes it such an insidious trap. God is True and Independent Existence. He is the Real Everything. Indeed, that is the very best definition for God that human words can express. Now, if God is Everything, how can there be anything else? If I have my own existence, then God is not Everything. There's God and there's me. Says the ego, "Oh, God is great, and I am a tiny speck. But I exist too." In other words, God is not really *Everything*. But the definition of God is complete Oneness. Therefore, if He is everything but me, then He's not really God.

"Okay, so I'm a heretic," says the ego. "Excommunicate me." That is not the point. This isn't a theological debate. Theology does not even begin to come into it. We are talking about our lives and our existence. We cannot be true to ourselves and we cannot be in tune with Reality if we are obsessed with an illusory image of self.

If you can live that way, more power to you. But addicts cannot live that way. Addicts are obsessed with finding a solution, even when they don't really understand what the problem is.

Addicts are desperately trying to destroy the E.G.O. that is making their life miserable, and they are willing to lose everything and even die in the process.

All or Nothing

The Torah says, "There is nothing else beside Him . . . The Lord is God in heaven above, and upon the earth below; there is nothing else" (Deuteronomy 4:35, 39). These verses are often taken as a rejection of polytheism. However, the Torah doesn't say, "There are no other *gods* beside Him"—that's already covered in the second of the Ten Commandments prohibiting idol worship. Here it says, "There is *nothing* else beside Him" and "There is *nothing* else."

It cannot be that He is one thing and the world and we are something else. There are not multiple existences. There is but One Existence. As the Ba'al Shem Tov, founder of the Chasidic movement, used to say, "All is God, and God is all." God is not only the Master and Creator of the world. He *is* the world, for He is Everything.

The central prayer of Judaism is the *Shema*. "Hear, O Israel, the Lord is our God. The Lord is One." (Deuteronomy 6:4) It doesn't say, "The Lord is the one God." It says, "The Lord is *One*"—that is, complete Unity and Oneness. Nothing exists apart from Him. It is E.G.O that implicitly denies this fact and thus E.G.O. that separates us from our true and essential relationship with God.

When we realize that God is truly Everything, we are released from E.G.O., and likewise, when we let go of E.G.O., we feel how God is truly Everything. Most people would call this "enlightenment" or some other fancy word. The recovering addict calls it sobriety.

The Twelve-Step programs do not espouse any religious views of God. They do not require that members embrace any particular conception of a Higher Power. (In later chapters, we will, however, discuss implicitly theological statements made within the program.) But the program does clearly make at least one statement about the nature of God—that the One who has the power to help us recover from addiction is Everything. To quote:

> When we became alcoholics, crushed by a self-imposed crisis we could not postpone or evade, we had to fearlessly face the proposition that either God is everything or else He is nothing. God either is, or He isn't. What was our choice to be? (*Alcoholics Anonymous*, p. 53)

According to all that we have explained about the problem of addiction, it only makes sense that this must be our concept of God.

The recovering addict can choose to call God whatever he or she wishes (which may be particularly important for one who was soured by negative religious experiences in the past), but ultimately, at least in my humble opinion, the whole idea of choosing one's own concept of God is little more than semantics. God is Everything, or else He is nothing. As long as one clings to E.G.O.—read: the belief in oneself as a separate existence independent from God—one cannot let God be God. And if God isn't God, then who will be? Who will take care of *me*? "I will," says E.G.O., "I always take care of myself." And *that* is when all hell breaks loose.

Fortunately, the addict does not have to be able to clearly understand any of this in order to recover. All that is necessary is to begin to let go of E.G.O. and as that obstacle is gradually diminished, the necessary God-consciousness will begin to take shape on its own.

PART II
THE SOLUTION

What exactly is the"spiritual solution"for recovery from addiction? How does it work? And can we explain why?

CHAPTER 4
HOW IT WORKS (NOT WHY)

A Recovery Parable

An addict is driving along all alone in his car one night on an empty highway. He is depressed beyond words, thinking how miserable he is and how he would do anything to get sober and have a normal life. Suddenly, as he's zooming down the highway and thinking, he hears the voice of God.

"I hear you're looking for sobriety," says God.

"Yes," he says, in awe.

"Well, you're in luck today," says God, "Because I happen to have sobriety, and it can be yours for a reasonable price."

"How much?"

"How much have you got?"

"I've got twenty dollars in my pocket."

"You're in luck," says God. "The price of sobriety today happens to be exactly twenty dollars."

"But that's everything I've got," the man protests, "If I give you all of my money, how will I buy gas for the car?"

"A car?" says God, "Oh, I see. The price of sobriety is twenty bucks and your car."

"But if I give you my car, how will I get to work tomorrow?"

"Work?" says God, "You have a job? The price of sobriety is twenty bucks, your car, and your job."

"But if I give you my job, then I won't get paid. I need to pay the mortgage this week."

"A mortgage? You mean you have a house? I hate to tell you this but the price of sobriety just went up. It's twenty bucks, your car, your job, and your house."

"But where will my family live?"

"Family? You've got a wife and kids? The price of sobriety is twenty bucks, your car, your job, your house, and your wife and kids."

At this point the man decides to shut up.

"Are you willing to take it?" asks God.

The man nods. God takes everything, and He is about to give the man his sobriety.

"But one thing," says God, "Before I give you your sobriety, there's something else I want you to do for me."

The man nods again.

"See this twenty dollars?" says God, "It's not your twenty dollars. It's My twenty dollars. You know that. But I want you to take it from Me, and I want you to be My emissary to spend it as I would. And you see this car? It's not your car. It's My car. But I want you to use it as I would. And this job, I want you to go to work and earn a paycheck. But it's not your job. It's My job. And I want you to behave there as I would. And this family—this wife and these kids. They're not your family. They're My family. But I want you to take care of them for me the way that I would. Can you do all of that?"

The man nods again.

"Then here it all is. And here is your sobriety."

Recovery in a Nutshell

So, that's basically recovery in a nutshell: addict gets tired of trying to make everything work; addict gives up and lets Higher Power take over; addict experiences unusual freedom, happiness, and usefulness as long as and to the extent that addict does not renege on previous decision.

I am sure that people who suffer from other conditions that are also incurable, progressive, and fatal would be thrilled if their diseases could be treated just as easily. It almost seems too good to be true, and it would be . . . *if* everybody who needed the solution knew about it *and* everyone who knew about it actually used it. But the irony of addiction is, as many people in recovery are apt to point out, that it is the disease that tells you don't have a disease.

Another way of putting it is that when you are full of yourself, it's very hard to see that you are the problem.

Or, conversely, when you need God the most, God is the last thing you want.

There's not much more to recovery than that the addict just follows some basic rules of living and is relieved from the obsession to use. It sounds like a neat trick. But as the old slogan goes, "There is no magic in recovery; just miracles."

This is a crucial point, one that we need to clarify right here and now if we are to understand how this program works.

People don't make miracles.

God does.

The addict's role in recovery is thus really no more than to just *get out of the way* so that God can make recovery happen.

If that sounds like some kind of voodoo or imaginary magic bullet, just remember how much incredibly hard work it actually takes to get out of the way.

If it were really so easy to let God do His business, then addicts wouldn't need to resort to numbing themselves into oblivion in a desperate attempt to replicate this effect. Would they? If we could all just snap our fingers and become selfless, we wouldn't need to follow a program that trains us how to live in harmony with God; we'd already just being doing it. So do not be mistaken: recovery is hard work—just not in the sense that we often think of it.

Not Self-Help, God-Help

To wit, a major misconception about the Twelve Steps is that they are a "self-help program." I've actually heard mental health professionals, albeit not ones who specialize in addiction, refer to the Twelve Steps as such. This description is completely inaccurate. The Twelve Steps are the very *opposite* of self-help.

*Active addiction is **self-help*** ("I take care of myself the only way I know how, because no one else can or will"). *Recovery is **God-help*** ("I can't continue trying to do for myself what only God can really do for me"). If one is a true addict in the sense described in the preceding chapters, then one will not recover by trying to get his or her own addiction under control. By the time one is an addict, there is no human power that can make the addiction go away. Addiction must be treated by a miracle. And as we said, miracles are God's business.

Now, here is an insightful question that a person of faith might ask at this point. From a Jewish perspective, how are the Twelve Steps any different from all other forms of healing? As the Torah explains, medical treatment is just a way of opening a natural pathway for God's healing powers to reach us in a nonmiraculous way. Thus, in essence, isn't it always God who does the work and we who just make room for Him, as the old saying goes, "God heals the patient and the doctor collects the fee"?

True. In that sense, recovery really is no different from any other kind of healing.

On the other hand, recovery is unique in that it cuts out the middle-man, so to speak. There are no pills and no therapies. Recovery is faith healing in the truest sense. Recovery is about opening yourself to God so that God can do whatever He needs to do with you so that you can best live your life.

Nevertheless, we must be clear about one thing. The reason we can treat addiction with straight spirituality, whereas we cannot use the same treatment for, say, a broken leg, is due to the very nature of the disease in the first place. As explained in the preceding chapters, addiction itself is an essentially spiritual malady and thus treatable by the application of overtly spiritual practices.

It Works If You Work It

To sum up what we've said so far in this chapter:

- The addict's work in recovery is simply to apply some basic rules of living.
- The addict is not really treating the condition so much as *allowing* treatment to ensue.
- The way this works is by following a program that is deceptively easy to describe.

Now ... *why* this works is another story altogether. I don't know why it works. Thus, the title of this part of the book, "The Solution," may actually be a bit misleading.

When we speak about the solution, all we mean is to identify:

- The precise means by which this solution is implemented (i.e., how do you do it); and
- The general goal the solution is meant to achieve (i.e., what happens when you do).

This doesn't mean that we know why it works. If you were to ask me to tell you *why* the Steps work, I would have to admit that I have no idea. I mean, to be honest, I think I have some general notion as to why they are effective. They train a person to get away from ego and become available for a conscious relationship with God, thereby alleviating the obsession with self-destruction as a means for relieving existential discomfort.

But I do not know why precisely it has to be these Steps or why they are in this order. I don't know why people who stick to the program succeed and those who don't take it seriously seem to have a much harder go of it. I don't know why the Steps don't seem to work as well when they are substituted, skipped, or modified.

I also don't know why the Steps are so completely life-transforming.

But I don't believe that anybody really knows any of this. All we know is that those who honestly commit themselves to the program find themselves utterly changed, and that this change is far more profound than mere chemical sobriety. Indeed, as we have already explained, in order to work, it would have to be.

Recovery folks often tell one another, "Keep coming back. It works if you work it." In other words, the people whose lives have already been transformed by the program can't really give fellow sufferers any better advice than, "Do what I did and you'll get the same results I got." They can't tell you *why* it works. All they know is that their lives today are testimony to the fact that it *does*.

Those who are familiar with recovery know that there is a chapter in the Big Book entitled "How It Works." In that chapter, the Twelve Steps are first enumerated and explained. It took me a while to consciously appreciate that the chapter is called "*How* It Works," not "*Why* It Works." The original architects of the Twelve Steps didn't pretend that they understood why these principles were so effective. All they knew, and all we know today, is that the program works.

Natural Law

It is my personal belief—and this is the theologian in me talking now—that the Steps work because they conform to certain basic, immutable laws of the universe. "You do this, you get that." In other words, the

Steps are not arbitrary any more than that which constitutes a healthy diet is arbitrary. Certain lifestyles promote health, and certain lifestyles do not. Just as there are laws of biology that determine what is healthy eating for the body, there are laws of spirituality that determine what is healthy living for the soul. One need not understand either of these types of laws to live in accordance with them.

For instance, you don't have to be a nutritionist to know that if for some crazy reason you go off and eat nothing but waffles for every meal, you are going to ruin your health. You can believe others when they tell you this, or you can try it on your own, but one way or another, you will come to the same conclusion as all other normal people. And you don't have to know *why* it is that way; you just know that it is.

If we look at recovery as a set of instructions for living according to the rules of life, I think it helps us also understand the challenge facing the addict. The addict is a person in desperate need of learning how to live.

Let's go back to the universal law that says that if you eat waffles all day, you'll get sick. A little kid who has a chance to eat nothing but waffles all day might actually try to do it. But that's normal. A little kid still needs to test things out. A normal adult, on the other hand, won't try it because a normal adult already knows, whether from personal experience, from watching others, or from logical deduction that the all-waffle diet won't work.

Now, let's apply this same concept to other areas of life besides eating. Certain emotional habits are unhealthy. Little kids need to experiment with unhealthy behaviors—like pouting, throwing tantrums, lying, and so forth—and try them on for size. As they grow up, however, they form conclusions and gradually cross certain behaviors off the list. By the time a person is mature, there are just certain routines that are no longer part of the repertoire. You don't fall on the ground and cry anymore when someone else gets the last piece of cake.

For whatever reason, addicts usually have not learned these lessons. It's not that addicts are unintelligent. To the contrary, they can be very smart and, indeed, prone to being unusually philosophical even if they are of average intelligence. If an addict had just two brain cells left, one would be trying to figure out how to kill the other one by getting wasted, while the other would be contemplating the meaning of life.

At any rate, addicts as a whole are not at all stupid. Yet, when it comes to living, they are inexplicably inept. There are certain life lessons that they have never grasped—the emotional equivalents of "don't eat waffles all day unless you want to get sick." As time goes by, rather than learning how to do what everyone else does, the addict increasingly overcompensates by developing an entire alternative set of life skills of dubious distinction such as a masterly knack for self-deception or an instinctive ability to manipulate others.

What the Twelve Steps seem to do is take grownups who are bad at life and train them to live as if they had learned the lessons we are all supposed to have learned from our early experiences. The Steps do not teach what the laws of the universe are. (As I said, I don't think the authors of the program necessarily even knew what they were.) The Steps do train a person, however, to live in a way that is in harmony with these laws.

The Science of Spirituality

I suppose one could ask how a bunch of ne'er-do-wells were able to devise a program that teaches people how to live in harmony with immutable laws of the universe.

My personal take on this is that the Twelve Steps were not invented so much as they were *discovered*. The Steps were the sum total of real experience gained through a process of much painful trial and error where the stakes were quite literally life and death. By seeing what worked—that is, by what principles an addict could actually *live*—the original members of the fellowship came to understand some basic rules for living. Thereby, they were able to arrive at certain irreducible needs of human spirituality.

In other words, those who developed the program did not set out to create a new religion or a new sect of a pre-existing one. They were searching for the most basic and universal spiritual truths—not through philosophical investigation but by actual experimentation. That is a *very* important distinction. In this sense, the Steps are actually closer to science than religion. Religion is based on revelation while science is based on empirical findings. Yes, the Steps are spiritual. But they are spiritual principles determined by seeing what actually works. The Steps are, if you will, a scientific study and application of spirituality.

This, by the way, answers a question that troubles many of my fellow Jews who ask how I can attribute such validity to a spiritual program that does not come from Torah.

The Midrash says, "If a person should tell you there is wisdom among the nations, believe it . . . But if he tells you there is Torah among the nations, do not believe it." We must distinguish between wisdom and Torah. Wisdom refers to human insight while Torah is Godly revelation. The Jews hold no monopoly on human insight. But it is foundational to our belief that we uniquely received the Torah from God at Sinai.

The Twelve Steps are not Torah. But they most certainly are wisdom. The fact that they are the product of human experience and experimentation does not lessen their validity as a tried and true way of life but, to the contrary, only strengthens it.

I have heard Jews in recovery say that they believe the Steps were written under "divine inspiration." I am not part of this camp. Firstly, I am not qualified to determine what is or is not divine inspiration—a term which our tradition uses quite rarely to describe only a very particular state of consciousness. Secondly, I find such a proclamation wholly unnecessary when we can just as easily rely upon the definitive ruling of the great 12th century philosopher and legalist, Maimonides, who said:"Accept the truth regardless of its source."

The Canary in the Coal Mine

Again, I feel compelled to remark that this is just my personal take on things, but I view the process of discovering the Steps as being very much like the way that miners of old would use a canary to test the air in the coal mine. In the days before mineshafts had proper ventilation, miners would bring a canary in a cage down with them whenever forging into a new area of the mine. Canaries are more sensitive to poisonous gasses than human beings, so as long as the canary was alive, the miners knew the air in the new area was safe to breathe. If the canary stopped singing, the miners knew it was time to get out of that part of the mine.

The canary was not a toxicologist, or whatever expert you would consult in order to determine whether or not air is safe to breathe. A canary is just a bird—a bird that when it breathes poison happens to die quicker than a human.

The early pioneers of recovery were the subjects of their own experimentation because they had to be. Those who survived saw what did and did not work. If a certain idea or practice is spiritually harmful to human beings, the addict would be the first to show symptoms. If a certain idea or practice promotes spiritual wellness in human beings, it would be evident in the addict by his or her relief from the compulsion to use.

The Steps are just about as simple as that. Let's take a closer look now at what they actually say.

CHAPTER 5
THE STEPS WE TOOK

Before the Book

In the early years of AA (1935–39), before the Big Book was written, the fellowship practiced a handful of simple ideas that were handed down orally from one member to another. Essentially, they learned the program from one another and guided one another in its implementation. However, as the effectiveness of the program became established and the fellowship prepared to expand its horizons, it was deemed necessary to put the basic principles in writing so that even those who did not have the advantage of one-on-one contact with the original members would be able to grasp the program.

Toward this end, a book was written.

It was cofounder Bill Wilson who was assigned the task of being the primary author, although, as it should already be clear, he was acting more as a scribe than as an innovator. The program was already in practice; it just needed to be put into the right words.

When Bill got to the chapter called "How It Works," he wanted to set out the basics of the program in a very simple format. Until then, there had never been any official concept of "Steps," let alone twelve of them. However, as mentioned in an earlier chapter, Bill had received from his friend Ebby some basic ideas about spirituality that Ebby in turn had taken from the Oxford Group. There were six main tenets, although they weren't officially numbered or even written down anywhere. We'll repeat them again now:

We admitted we were licked.
We got honest with ourselves.
We talked it over with another person.
We made amends to those we had harmed.
We tried to carry this message to others with no thought of reward.
We prayed to whatever God we thought there was.

It is interesting to note that according to one early AA member's auto-biographical account, Dr. Bob Smith also conveyed six basic principles to newcomers. As the author remembers, these ideas were like a prototype for the Twelve Steps. They were:

1. Complete deflation
2. Dependence and guidance from a Higher Power
3. Moral inventory
4. Confession
5. Restitution
6. Continued work with other alcoholics (*Alcoholics Anonymous*, p.263)

We see many of the same themes in both the list of points that Ebby transmitted to Bill and the version taught by Dr. Bob. (See the table on p. 46.) "We admitted we were licked" is pretty much the same as "complete deflation," which leads to "dependence and guidance from a Higher Power." These ideas were to form the basis for the first three Steps.

"We got honest with ourselves" may be a part of the initial surrender and thus, related to Steps 1-3, but it may also be a part of taking an un-flinching look at one's own character, in which case, it's the same as "moral inventory," in which case it is the basis for Step Four.

"We talked it over with another person" is the same as "confession" which is the same as what would become Steps 5-7.

"We made amends to those we had harmed" is the same as "restitu-tion." This is the main idea of what we know today to be Steps Eight and Nine.

"We tried to carry this message to others with no thought of reward" is the same as "continued work with other alcoholics" which is part of Step Twelve.

"We prayed to whatever God we thought there was," which is Step Eleven, isn't mentioned clearly in the second list, but we can see from the author's description (*ibid.*) of how Dr. Bob actually took him through the process that prayer was not only mentioned but also was a major empha-sis.

We see that early AA was not about the precise words but the actions they took. And that worked just fine as long as newcomers could learn from those who had already begun working the program successfully themselves. However, if the program was to be able to transcend the limits of geographical proximity as well as stand the test of time, then there would have to be some form of codification of its most basic principles.

Bill would later recall that he had at first had a very difficult time with this task:

> I was in this anything-but-spiritual mood on the night when the Twelve Steps of Alcoholics Anonymous were written. I was sore and tired clear through. I lay in bed at 182 Clinton Street with pencil in hand and with a tablet of scratch paper on my knee. I could not get my mind on the job, much less put my heart in it. But here was one of those things that had to be done....
>
> Finally I started to write. I set out to draft more than six steps; how many more I did not know. I relaxed and asked for guidance. With a speed that was astonishing, considering my jangling emotions, I completed the first draft. It took perhaps half an hour. The words kept right on coming. When I reached a stopping point, I numbered the new steps. They added up to twelve. (*AA Comes of Age*, pp. 160–161)

Bill submitted his manuscript for review by the other members, who suggested certain changes. After incorporating their edits, the Steps took on the form by which they are recognized today:

Here are the steps we took, which are suggested as a program of recovery:

1. We admitted we were powerless over alcohol—that our lives had become unmanageable.
2. Came to believe that a Power greater than ourselves could restore us to sanity.
3. Made a decision to turn our will and our lives over to the care of God *as we understood Him*.
4. Made a searching and fearless moral inventory of ourselves.
5. Admitted to God, to ourselves, and to another human being the exact nature of our wrongs.
6. Were entirely ready to have God remove all these defects of character.

7. Humbly asked Him to remove our shortcomings.
8. Made a list of all persons we had harmed, and became willing to make amends to them all.
9. Made direct amends to such people wherever possible, except when to do so would injure them or others.
10. Continued to take personal inventory and when we were wrong promptly admitted it.
11. Sought through prayer and meditation to improve our conscious contact with God *as we understood Him*, praying only for knowledge of His will for us and the power to carry that out.
12. Having had a spiritual awakening as the result of these steps, we tried to carry this message to alcoholics, and to practice these principles in all our affairs." (*Alcoholics Anonymous*, p. 59)

Ebby's Points to Bill	Corresponding Steps	Dr. Bob's Version	Corresponding Steps
We admitted we were licked.	1, 2, and 3	Complete deflation	1
We got honest with ourselves.	1 or 4	Dependence and guidance from a Higher Power	2, 3
We talked it over with another person.	5	Moral inventory	4
We made amends to those we had harmed.	8, 9	Confession	5, 6, 7
We tried to carry this message to others with no thought of reward.	12	Restitution	8, 9
We prayed to whatever God we thought there was.	11	Continued work with other alcoholics	12

Alternative Renditions

A while ago, someone sent me an e-mail that was being forwarded around called "The Twelve Steps Made Simple." No doubt, some addict or addicts put it together and decided to share it with others.

I think it is especially enlightening for those who are unfamiliar with the program because it is written in a style that reveals what the Steps mean to someone who has actually worked them. Here they are:

The Twelve Steps Made Simple
1. There's a power that will kill me.
2. There's a power that wants me to live.
3. Which do I want? (If you want to die, stop here. If you want to live, go on.)
4. Using examples from your own life, understand that selfishness, dishonesty, resentment, and fear control your actions.
5. Tell all your private, embarrassing secrets to another person.
6. Decide whether or not you want to live that way any more.
7. If you want your life to change, ask a Power greater than yourself to change it for you. (If you could have changed it yourself, you would have long ago.)
8. Figure out how to make right all the things you did wrong.
9. Fix what you can without causing more trouble in the process.
10. Understand that making mistakes is part of being human. (When you make a mistake, fix it, immediately if you can.)
11. Ask for help to treat yourself and others like you the way you want your Higher Power to treat you.
12. Don't stop doing 1 through 11, and pass it on.

Equally edifying, and even more entertaining, is this little stroke of brilliance someone devised entitled "The Twelve Steps of Insanity." Here, the anonymous author reveals the essence of each Step—and, indeed, the essence of the program, I think—by turning the entire program on its head.

Notice how this parody makes it clear that the central and defining conflict in recovery is between God and ego, the selfless and the selfish. By getting away from ego, one gets better; by becoming wrapped up in ego, one does the exact opposite:

The Twelve Steps Of Insanity

1. We admitted we were powerless over nothing—that we could manage our lives perfectly and those of anyone who would let us.
2. Came to believe that there was no power greater than ourselves and the rest of the world was insane.
3. Made a decision to have our loved ones turn their wills and their lives over to our care even though they could not understand us at all.
4. Made a searching and fearless moral inventory of every one we knew.
5. Admitted to the world the exact nature of everyone else's wrongs.
6. Were entirely ready to make others give us the respect we so rightfully deserved.
7. Demanded that others do our will because we were always right.
8. Made a list of all persons who had harmed us and became willing to go to any lengths to get even with them.
9. Got direct revenge on such people wherever possible except when to do so would cost us our lives or at the very least a jail sentence.
10. Continued to take inventory of others and when they were wrong, promptly and repeatedly told them about it.
11. Sought through complaining and medication to improve our relations with others, as we would not understand them at all, asking only that they do things our way.
12. Having had a complete physical, emotional, and spiritual breakdown as a result of these steps, we blamed it on others and tried to get sympathy and pity in all our affairs.

Finally, I'd like to share with you this little jewel of insight and brevity.

Somebody from the program went and distilled each Step down to one word. This list, like the two above, is certainly not definitive, just one person's take. But again, it's very helpful in understanding the true spirit of the program.

Each Step in a Word

1. Honesty
2. Hope

3. Faith
4. Courage
5. Truth
6. Willingness
7. Humility
8. Accountability
9. Justice
10. Integrity
11. God-consciousness
12. Service

The Program in Six Words

Of course, if we are really looking to sum up the Steps, we shouldn't fail to mention the "Twelve Steps in Six Words" formula that is often attributed to AA cofounder Dr. Bob Smith :

Trust God.
Clean House.
Help Others.

Corresponding to the Steps as they are numbered, it looks something like this:

Two-Word Action	Step(s)
Trust God.	1–3
Clean House.	4–11
Help Others.	12

In Jewish tradition, trust in God is called *bittachon*, which literally means "confidence" or "security." It means that one trusts in God to the extent that one feels certain that everything will be taken care of in the best possible way.

Housecleaning is known as *cheshbon ha-nefesh*—literally, "spiritual stocktaking." This includes the process of honestly appraising one's character and becoming willing to rectify one's faults.

Helping others is the concept of *tzedakah*—often mistranslated as "charity" but really meaning "justice." Acting charitably means doing something you really don't have to do, whereas justice means fulfilling a duty. Fulfilling commandments such as "You shall surely open your hand to your brother" (Deuteronomy 15:11) or "Do not stand idly by your neighbor's blood" (Leviticus 19:16) is not simply a nice thing to do. It's an obligation.

These three ideas are the program in a nutshell. In Part III, the section that now follows, we will take a closer look at the Steps with a specific eye toward gleaning any information that may indicate more about the underlying theological beliefs of the program.

PART III
A THEOLOGICAL STUDY
OF THE TWELVE STEPS

Despite their being officially nondenominational, do the Steps make any statements, explicit or implied, indicating certain beliefs? If so, are these beliefs compatible with Torah?

A Rabbi's Perspective

In spite of everything we've spoken of so far pointing to the universal truths behind the spiritual principles of recovery, I am sure that for many readers the nagging question remains—"Okay, sure, the Twelve Steps aren't *officially* Christian, but are they really compatible with my beliefs as a Jew?"

At least, that is how I have heard the question posed to me hundreds of times.

My first answer is that I cannot tell anyone whether the Steps can be reconciled with their personal beliefs because I don't know exactly what it is that any one person believes. All I can attempt to do is try to show how the Steps fit—or don't fit—with Jewish *belief*, which does not necessarily have to be the same as what the individual asking the question may or may not *believe*. So let us establish from the start, I am not trying to tell anyone what to believe—not as a Jew and not as a recovering person. What I *can* do is look at the Steps from a theological perspective, as a rabbi and a student of the Torah, and offer my best analysis of what the Steps seem to be telling us about their approach to relating to God.

How Jewish Are the Steps?

There's an easy way to avoid answering this question altogether. That is just to say that since the Steps espouse no particular theological beliefs, they are, as such, compatible with all spiritual paths.

I don't like that answer.

I don't think that it's completely accurate or completely honest. The Steps, although replete with the qualifier, "God of our understanding," *do* make, or at least *imply*, some definite theological assertions. It's impossible to talk that much about God without having at least some unspoken presuppositions about who exactly this God is.

The answer I usually give is not only that there is nothing in the Twelve Steps that is problematic from a Jewish perspective, but also that the Steps can actually help Jews to better understand their own God. The Steps, in their clear and simple language, marvelously communicate certain truths in which we as Jews are already enjoined to believe. Accordingly, as expressed in the title of this book, the Jew in recovery is often delighted to find that the "God of our understanding" turns out to be the very same as "the God of our father."

At the same time, I humbly try to keep in mind the story of the alcoholic Quaker who, after having sobered up in AA, wrote to Bill Wilson to tell him that the Steps were remarkably consistent with the beliefs he had already gained from his religious background. Wilson responded, in a now published letter (*As Bill Sees It*, p. 116): "The really amazing fact about AA is that all religions see in our program a resemblance to themselves."

So, at last, whether the Steps more closely represent one belief system or another is irrelevant. I have no stake in calling the Steps *Jewish* even if they strike me as being such. What I do feel is important, however, is to explain my understanding of the Steps in a way that can potentially help Jews feel comfortable, knowing that their recovery through the Twelve Steps does not compromise their Jewishness in any way. This, in many ways, is actually the whole point of this book—*to help Jewish addicts find recovery through the Steps*.

I am aware of the argument that what I am doing here is unnecessary. There are those who will dismiss the need for a Jewish commentary on recovery because, as they explain, a Jew need not see the Steps as Jewish in order to make use of them. When in need of healing, they say, Judaism enjoins us to use whatever means are effective. Just as a Jew does not require a uniquely Jewish method of treating his or her medical problems, so, too, a Jew does not need a uniquely Jewish method of recovering from addiction.

The problem with this argument is that the Steps are not your conventional medicine or therapy, even though it would simplify things a great deal if we claimed that they were. The Steps are a prescription for a spiritual way of living. Accordingly, we Jews rightfully wonder whether this spiritual way of life is consistent with our tradition.

What Does "Nondenominational" Really Mean?

At the risk of making a sweeping generalization, allow me to say that addicts are always looking for an excuse not to recover. It's part of the disease. Every addict—irrespective of his or her drug of choice—possesses a certain nagging sense of what we call "terminal uniqueness." Eventually, the addict will always claim, "But my case is different." It's not so much that addicts are too proud to buy into anything too "mainstream"—although that is certainly a factor. Rather, addicts typically feel so unusual, so special, that they have difficulty believing that anything normal, popular, or universal can be of any help to them.

This presents a special dilemma. The premise of Twelve Steps recovery is that living according to basic spiritual principles brings a reprieve from active addiction. Spirituality, as we have discussed previously, is the solution. But if the Twelve Steps were recognizably aligned to any known ideology or set of beliefs, addicts would find an easy excuse for feeling driven away from the program. Thus we see that while Twelve-Step groups are, as a rule, staunchly committed to spiritual principles, they are equally as renowned for their flexibility on all matters pertaining to the particular beliefs of their members. Indeed, one criticism leveled at Twelve-Step fellowships by religiously inclined individuals, both from within and outside of the program, is the perceived ambiguity as to what beliefs are actually set forth by the spiritual tenets of recovery.

In recovery circles, one often hears this dichotomy described as the distinction that we have noted before between spirituality and religion. Religion denotes dogma and the default acceptance of certain articles of faith, whereas spirituality is a softer, suppler word that leaves itself open for all kinds of interpretation. To wit, there is the widely told, though perhaps apocryphal, tale of the agnostic who upon coming to AA decided to choose the doorknob as his Higher Power.

For the reason we have just discussed, it is understandable that AA and the Twelve Step groups that came after it have held a staunchly nonsectarian position on matters of belief. At the same time, however, it would be dishonest to claim that the Steps are devoid of any theology. While there is nothing like a list of theological principles where tenets of faith are enumerated, a thoughtful reading of the Steps will lead one to conclude that they are indeed based on and espouse a distinct theological position.

In other words, subtlety should not be confused with neutrality. There is a consistent theology to the Twelve Steps and to pretend otherwise would be to ignore the very Power upon which they draw to facilitate the recovery of the addict.

Of course, the question that now arises is, as we have noted: How is this theology compatible with Judaism?

In the chapters that follow, we will take a deeper look, from a Jewish perspective, at what the Steps are actually saying about God.

The "God Steps"

Four of the Steps (3, 5, 6, and 11) explicitly mention God and two more of them refer to God indirectly, either as "a Power greater than ourselves" (Step Two) or by the pronoun "Him" (Step Seven).

The use of the word "God" four times throughout the Steps—a work that contains only about two hundred words—constitutes a ubiquitous usage. (Indeed, excluding any pronouns, prepositions, and definite or indefinite articles, God is *the* most repeated word in the Steps.) As such, it's difficult to imagine that the Steps do not offer some notion of who or what this God is. Moreover, although, as mentioned earlier, it often serves a convenient purpose to act as if the program takes no distinct theological position, to persist in this assertion is simply to discount the facts.

The Steps don't just refer to God, they also tell us about Him. First, they let us know that He is a Power, and that this Power is greater than ourselves. God is not an idea or an abstraction. He is a force, and He is active. And this force is more powerful than we are. Further, we are told that this Power can actually do something for us—something quite big. It can "restore us to our sanity." These are all theological statements, and these are all contained just in Step Two. In other words, right away in the Second Step, we have already been told quite a lot about God—not just that He exists, but also about how He manifests Himself in our lives.

The next Step, in which we are told to turn our will and our lives to His care, tells us even more about God—He *cares*. That's another distinct theological position. One can believe in God and not believe that He cares, but this Step tells us, at least implicitly, that He does indeed care. In Step Five, we are told that we can talk to Him; we can speak to Him openly and honestly about ourselves. In Steps 6 and 7, we are told that God can change us, and that we can ask Him to do so. In Step Eleven, we are told that we can consciously engage Him, and that we can ask Him for knowledge of His will, and the power to carry out this will. This, incidentally, also sets forth another very big idea—God has a will. That's a strong theological statement. And not only does He have a will, but He has a will for *us*, things He specifically desires from the individual.

Hence, far from existing in a theological vacuum, the Steps actually convey several key ideas about God. These are not to be taken for granted. They are by no means universal to all systems of belief. Not all theologies hold these views, but the program does. He is a Power; He can affect our lives; He is caring; He has a will.

In the following chapters of this section, we will look at each of these very important ideas about God, how to see them in the Steps, and how they relate to Jewish belief.

With a Capital "P"

The first allusion to God in the Steps is found in Step Two, where He is referred to as "a Power greater than ourselves." Note the capitalization. It is evident that we are not just talking about any power that happens to be stronger than we are. If that were so, then the recovering person might choose to believe that gravity or electromagnetism could restore his or her sanity. Those powers are greater than we are. We certainly cannot defy their effects. But we also have no reason to believe that they can do anything for us other than blindly impose their influences as dictated by the laws of nature. When we speak about Power, that is, the proper (capitalized) rather than common (uncapitalized) noun, we are talking about a force that transcends *all* other powers in the universe.

The Zohar says, "Master of the Worlds, You are the Highest of the High, the Causer of Causes." Maimonides expresses much the same idea in his *Laws of the Foundations of the Torah*, albeit in a more philosophical tone, where he writes:

> [God] is the cause of all that exists . . . and there is no possibility that He does not exist, because without Him, all existence would cease. [Whereas] if we could imagine the absence of all existence other than His, the existence of God would not cease or diminish, for He is self-sufficient, and His existence requires nothing other than Himself."

In other words, although the phrase "Power greater than ourselves" may lend itself to being interpreted as any power the effects of which are unavoidable, if read in the context of the rest of the Steps, it is obvious that the "Power" mentioned in Step Two is not the sun or the ocean tides but the same God who is explicitly mentioned throughout—the God who restores sanity (Step Two), who cares for the individual (Step Three), who removes character defects (5, 6, and 7), and who lets His will be known and grants power to the individual to adhere to that will (Step Eleven).

Still more context will be of even greater help to us in understanding the Power alluded to in the Second Step. In the Big Book, just before the Steps are first enumerated, this idea is stated unambiguously:"Without help, it is too much for us. But there is One who has all power—that One is God. May you find Him now!" (p. 59). Clearly, when Step Two speaks of a Power, it does not mean just any power. It really means the "One." It means God.

Higher or Highest

One still might ask, if this Power is indeed singular and unique, if it is none other than the Power behind all other powers, then why is it referred to only as "*a* Power" (with the indefinite article) and not "*the* Power"?

Perhaps the following story will prove illuminating.

A well-known AA old-timer, Clancy I., talks about his early experiences grappling with belief. He relates how he told his sponsor that he could not believe in God. His sponsor asked him whether he could believe in the concept of God and just not use the word "God." Clancy said that he could not. The sponsor asked him whether he could believe in the power of the AA group. Clancy said that he could not manage to do that either. Finally, the sponsor asked him, "Can you admit that I am doing better than you?" Clancy said that he could. "Congratulations, kid," said the sponsor, "You've just met your new Higher Power."

More telling than the story itself is its epilogue. Years later, Clancy's sponsor stopped working the program, got drunk, and died. What was Clancy to do now, what with his "Higher Power" being dead and all? Would he lose his direction, his faith? Not at all. As Clancy explains it, by the time he lost his sponsor, Clancy already believed in God. It was his belief in his sponsor as *a* power greater than himself that was the necessary first move *away* from self-reliance. Once he was able to accept his dependence upon something outside of his own ego, he had already begun his journey toward finding God.

In other words, it is most probably safe to say that a person can get sober and work an effective Second Step just by believing in *any* power.

Indeed, it is often the case that belief in a higher power—any higher power!—is that which marks the nascent beginnings of a process toward discovering the *Highest* Power. It is the *Highest* Power that is referred to explicitly in the following Steps, which come right out and unambiguously invoke the word "God." Therefore, while Step Two does not tell us that we need to believe in God per se, it most certainly begins to lead us in that direction.

I once heard an Al-Anon speaker share a story about a friend of hers, an avowed atheist, who could not "come to believe" and take Step Two. One day, she was sitting in her kitchen and looking out her window while bemoaning the fact that she could in no way bring herself to believe in any power great than herself. Her rational mind just wouldn't allow it. Suddenly, she took notice of a great oak tree that grew on the property, and she began to think, "I could not make that oak tree. That oak tree must be a power greater than myself." That was her conclusion, and so she began talking to the oak tree, pouring her heart out to the oak tree in times of distress. And she felt better. Well, there came a day when she moved away from that house and had to leave the oak tree behind. She had been years in recovery by that time and had been pouring her heart out to the oak tree and now she would have to leave it behind. What happened next, however, left her delighted and surprised. As she said, "I left that house and the oak tree stayed behind. But what do you know? God came with me."

The point of these stories is *not*—perish the thought!—to endorse hero-worship or animism as a steppingstone to belief in God. Heaven forbid! What I am merely trying to point out is that for *all of us*, belief is a process. For some, it begins by making only the smallest possible concessions that the rational mind can bare. But if one is honest and one continues seeking, one *will* find true faith in the end.

In a way, such an evolution of faith is similar to the physicist who searches for a Unifying Theory of Everything that would fully explain and connect all known physical phenomena and forces of nature. A scientist looks at gravity, electromagnetism, and the nuclear forces and notes their power. However, the question remains, is there a power beyond those powers? And if so, is there a power that is beyond that power too?

This method of arriving at faith in God through a gradual process of deduction was exemplified by the spiritual quest of the world's first champion of monotheism, Abraham. As Maimonides describes in the first chapter of his *Laws Concerning the Prohibition of Idolaltry*:

[Abraham] was but a small child when his mind began to seek and wonder, "How do the heavenly bodies orbit without a moving force? Who moves them? They cannot move themselves!" . . . His heart sought and then came to know that there is but one God . . . who created all and that in all existence there is none other than He."

Abraham discovered belief in the One God through a process of looking *further and further outside* of himself until arriving at "The Causer of Causes." When we begin to look beyond our own ego, we have already begun our journey to find God. The unfortunate fact of the matter, however, is that many of us stop short in our quest. We find belief in something beyond ourselves and rest on our spiritual laurels. In recovery, however, one does not have the luxury of spiritual stagnation. One's faith must continuously grow. Certainly, for a Jew the belief in the Highest Power, and not just any power, is essential to our faith. We may begin, like Abraham, by searching somewhere "out there," anywhere beyond the self, but we must always arrive at the realization that ultimately there is *One* who has *all* power, and that *One* is God.

The Unwritten God in the First Step

This idea of looking for power beyond one's own ego is the content of Step One in which the addict admits his or her own powerlessness. Thus, in a very important way, the process of finding God as Highest Power subtly begins before Step Two has even introduced the notion of a Higher Power. In other words, before we can begin to honestly look for God as a Power, we have to admit our own limitations. As is often said in recovery circles, "There is a God . . . and you are not Him."

It might be useful to note that Chasidus teaches that the opposite of serving God is not idolatry but the service of self. At least idolaters turn to an entity outside of themselves whereas egomaniacs—and addicts, almost by definition, fit that profile—cannot peacefully defer to anyone or anything aside from their own egos. Thus, the mental shift that is most critical and urgent is that of the addict's adherence to the simple piece of advice often heard in the rooms: "Get out of your own head."

The Talmud relates that God says of an arrogant person, "It is impossible for him and Me to dwell in the same place." Although God is omnipresent, His Presence cannot be felt where there is haughtiness and pride. To allow the Power of God into one's life, one must first acquiesce to the fact of his or her own lack of power. The story is told that when the famed Chasidic master, Rabbi Menachem Mendel Morgensztern of Kotzk was but a small child he was asked, "Where is God?" to which the young rabbi-to-be replied, "Wherever you let Him in." This same idea is expressed by the midrashic saying, "You cannot pour into a cup that is already full."

In other words, God will always fill whatever space we make for Him but He will not intrude where He is clearly unwelcome. In order to experience God's Power in Step Two, one first makes a "power vacuum" in Step One. This recognition of the limits of personal power sets the scene for entering into a relationship with that which is Unlimited Power.

God Almighty

If in Step One you become ready to meet God, then in Step Two, you actually meet Him. But why does the first reference to God in the Steps allude to Him as "Power"?

One might answer that since "God" is a word fraught with so many connotations and one that evokes so many prejudices, it just works better to ease into it and not to use the word "God" right away. This is a valid point. For many people, "God" can be a "scare word," as in the old Jewish tale of the rabbi who tells the atheist, "My son, don't worry. The same God that you don't believe in, I don't believe in either."

But this still does not answer our question. Why allude to God specifically as a Power and not by any other word that one might also use to refer to God?

One might answer that since Step One calls for the individual to admit his or her own *lack of power*, it logically follows that Step Two should introduce God as the one who *has the power*. But there seems to be more to it than that.

There's a saying in recovery, "Don't tell God how big your addiction is; tell your addiction how big God is." The disease of addiction—regardless of drug of choice—is essentially an obsession with power. The addict wants control and finds it in the altering of his or her state by indulging in the addictive behavior. Hence, in order to recover, the addict must surrender this desire for control. But surrender it to what? To God? But what is

God? The likelihood that surrender will be effective as a means for treating addiction depends entirely on one's concept of God. Simply put, the idea that God can heal the addict only seems true if the God of one's conception is a God to whom one can worthily surrender one's own power. God may be many things to many people, but for the recovering addict, God must before all else be Power.

Indeed, this may be the reason that the practice of religion by itself is usually inadequate in treating addiction. One can believe in God and even practice some form of devotion to Him, but if one does not come to believe in God as Power, then there is nothing to which the addict can surrender control. While there may be many religions or belief systems that view God as the archetype of many such abstractions as Love, Wisdom, and Peace, in recovery God is the quintessence of Power and is introduced as such even before He is introduced by the name "God."

The medieval Jewish philosopher, Judah Ha-Levi, explains in *The Kuzari* why the first commandment of the Decalogue states, "I am the Lord your God, who took you out of Egypt." Why did God not introduce Himself as "The Lord your God, who created the heaven and the earth"? Surely that is a far more impressive credential. Ha-Levi answers that God chose to introduce Himself in the way that would be most relevant to those whom He was addressing. The concept of creation seems too abstract, dare we say, too impersonal, to serve as a basis of a relationship. The Exodus, on the other hand, demonstrated God's direct involvement in the affairs of man—that God did not just make the world, but that He is involved in it as well, and is all-powerful to act within it as He wishes. In other words, the Jewish relationship with God is not predicated upon God's role as Creator but as Power.

I once spoke to a young man who had been in and out of recovery for about a year and had not managed to put together any significant amount of clean time. He called me because he said that he needed to believe in a Higher Power but that he lacked the background to be able to figure out who or what that was. I asked him to describe for me the God of his understanding. He told me that, as he understood it, God was compassionate, just, and wise. I told him that, according to our tradition, all of those descriptions were apt, but that he had left out the most important one. He grappled, to no avail, to find the magic word that I was waiting to hear. I told him, "You say that you came to me because you wanted to find your

Higher *Power*. If your Higher *Power* is God, then why don't you mention that God is *powerful?*"

We began to discuss various mystical concepts that describe God's absolute control over the universe. Chasidus is replete with analogies and examples illustrating how God did not just create the world but that He continues to exert absolute control over every detail of reality. I told him about the Jewish mystical concept of "ongoing creation," that even now, God is bringing the universe into existence out of absolute void and nothing. As God continually creates something out of nothing, He places everything exactly where He wants it—at this very second. Without this constant imposition, all of creation would revert to nothingness. As such, there is no automatic pilot; God is always in control. In the lingo of recovery, "Nothing, absolutely nothing, happens in God's world by mistake" (*Alcoholics Anonymous*, p. 417).

Although he found our discussion intellectually stimulating, the young man stated that "in his heart," he could not bring himself to believe in this kind of omnipotence. I asked him, "What good is it to you to have a God who is compassionate, just, and wise if He is unable to exercise His compassion, justice, and wisdom whenever and however He likes? How can such a weakling restore you to your sanity, let alone be deemed worthy of having you give your life and will over to him?" The young man was open to many ideas about God but for whatever reason, he could not accept God as Power. The last I heard from him, he was still trying to figure out God—and he was still trying to get sober.

God cannot be an abstraction. We can describe Him with all the great and lofty terms we can think of, but if we cannot see Him as an active force in our lives, then we have not even begun to know what God is.

My teacher, the Lubavitcher Rebbe, of blessed memory, delivered most of his public addresses in Yiddish. But whenever he spoke in English, he would always refer to God with the somewhat unusual phrase "God Almighty"—though this was not a direct translation of the term for God that he most often used in his first language. There is something telling about this. When we speak of God—particularly in a secular language lacking an adequate lexicon for divine concepts—we must underscore that God is Power, that He is not just "God"—whatever that means to us—but "God Almighty."

CHAPTER 8
GOODNESS

God's Care

We have established that the God spoken of in the Steps is first and foremost a God of Power. But power does not necessarily convey beneficence. God may be strong, but is He good? In the Third Step, where we find the first use of the actual word "God," we also find the answer to this question. God is not just the epitome of power; He is the essence of goodness as well.

The Third Step enjoins us to "turn our will and our lives over to the *care* of God . . ." The word "care" is significant. Step Three is a surrender step—in recovery parlance what is called ""turning it over" or "letting go and letting God." In theory, one could just as well be enjoined to surrender to the *power* of God or to the *authority* of God. Were God only all-powerful and not also good, that would still provide amply sufficient cause to submit to Him. Yet, the Third Step adds a vital dimension to the recovering addict's concept of God. We "turn it over" to God not just because He is stronger than we are, but also because He will take better care of us than we can.

Jewish tradition discusses the idea that, at least in theory, God could have chosen to relate to us only as a Power. In reality, however, He chooses to relate to His creation from a position of kindness as well. The Midrash says, "At first, God had thought to create the world solely with the attribute of stern judgment. He foresaw, however, that the world would not endure that way and thus coupled with it the attribute of compassionate mercy." In other words, if God had created a world in which He were present only as a Higher Power but not as a source of caring, that world would not be able to last. Judaism sees a world in which God is all-powerful but not kind as an impossibility, nothing more than a hypothetical construct that cannot actually exist. In this light, the very existence of the world is in and of itself a testimony to the fact that God is not just powerful but also kind.

Knowing and Nurturing

The word "care" connotes two distinct but equally important meanings. One meaning of the word care is attentiveness. To care *about* something means to pay it mind, to be concerned. It is the opposite of indifference. Another meaning of care is nurturing. To care *for* something means to look after it. Thus, the word "care" implies both attentiveness *and* nurturing.

Let's first speak about God's attentiveness. When we say that God "pays attention," we are referring to his omniscience. "Does He that made the ear not hear? Does He that fashioned the eye not see?" (Psalms 94:9). If God is aware of anything, then He is aware of everything. For the Infinite, there is no such thing as having His attention divided or being preoccupied, overwhelmed, or distracted. It is axiomatic that the God who knows His creation knows every detail therein with intimate knowledge.

Maimonides goes as far as to consider this one of the most basic tenets of belief: "God knows the actions of people and does not ignore them. It is not like those who say (Ezekiel 8:12), 'God has abandoned the earth'" (*Principles of Faith*). Those who are aware of the historical context of Maimonides' writings know that this declaration of God's omniscience was a direct refutation of the popular thinking of the time that held that God was unconcerned with the affairs of man. This view of a lofty and aloof God was carried down from the philosophies of Plato and Aristotle, whose ideas still very much dominate Western attitudes of today. They believed that God's eternal unchangingness necessitates that He be completely unconcerned by a temporal world that is continuously in a state of flux. In other words, if God is unchanging, then how can He have a conscious relationship with that which is always changing? The Jewish view, in contrast, dismisses this as a nonargument. God's being Infinite and One does not exist *apart* from creation; rather creation exists *within* Him. As such, God, in knowing Himself, knows His creation. In the words of Maimonides (*Laws of the Foundations of the Torah*), "All existences besides the Creator—from the highest [spiritual] form to a tiny gnat in the belly of the earth—exist by virtue of His reality. In knowing His own reality, He thus knows everything."

In layman's terms: God does not need to be detached from His creation in order to be timeless. When God takes note of what is going on in the world, it's not like a person who gets caught up in counting the cracks in the ceiling tiles, and is mentally absorbed in something outside of himself. God pays attention to the world because the world exists within Him. He knows Himself thoroughly and thus, knows every aspect of His world.

This belief that God is always paying attention is crucial to recovery. In order to recover, we must be willing to do something that is very scary: We need to step aside from playing God in our own lives and place ourselves unreservedly in God's care. Program literature voices this sentiment in no uncertain terms. "Abandon yourself to God as you understand God" (*Alcoholic Anonymous*, p. 164). How could a person—particularly one who is so used to trying to control every aspect of life—possibly find peace by surrendering to a God who is indifferent or unknowing? The God who keeps the recovering addict sober, sane, and alive must be a God who can be counted on to care. And this care is not relegated to only some aspects of life. If one were to believe that God has limited or selective knowledge of His creation, then one could only release to God those things that one believes are relevant or interesting to Him. (And who could know a thing like that?) But the addict's recovery is based upon his or her freedom to turn *everything* over to the care of God and to do so without reservation. Surrender that is conditional, incomplete, or later reneged is deemed "taking back one's will"—a sort of anti–Third Step or Third Step in reverse, as it were, whereas the Third Step, taken properly, means a decision to trust that in all matters, God does, without a doubt, care.

This brings us to the second meaning of the word "care." As mentioned, caring also means *nurturing*. The idea of God as Caregiver is just as central to Judaism as any other conception of God, including that of Creator or King. Indeed, as noted above, a world without God's compassion and kindness could not exist. Furthermore, God's goodness is not just a necessary component of creation but also the underlying and primary impetus for its existence. As Kabbalah explains, God created the world "in order to bestow goodness upon His creations, for it is the nature of the Good to do good."

It is interesting that Judaism, particularly Kabbalah, uses blatantly feminine terminology to describe God's role as Nurturer, evoking images of God as a loving mother. The name for God's Immanent Presence, *Shechinah*, is unmistakably feminine. It is this name that is used in describing how the Divine Presence accompanies Her children wherever they go, even into the darkness of exile, as in the Talmud's statement: "See how beloved are Israel before God, for in every place where they were sent away, the *Shechinah* went with them."

When viewed in this light, the idea of giving oneself over to "the care of God" is one that evokes feelings of comfort, peace, and security—feelings that are pleasant for all people but essential for the person in recovery. It is said that addicts have little tolerance for discomfort, hence, the intensely felt reflex to self-medicate that can be triggered by the slightest feeling of uneasiness (or by none at all). The remarkable efficacy of spiritual consciousness as a means of recovery may in large part be explained by the serenity that it offers, which the addict needs so direly. This serenity is contingent upon a belief in a caring, nurturing God who always does good.

Everything Is Good

Combining what we have learned about God in Steps 2 and 3, we now have a "God of our understanding," who is—in theological parlance—omnipotent (Power), omniscient (cares about), and omnibenevolent (cares for). Now we are faced with a problem. If God is all-powerful, all-knowing, and all-good, then why is there suffering in the world? In other words, "Why do bad things happen to good people?" But this is hardly a novel question. Throughout the ages, much ink has been spilled in attempts at resolving this conundrum. Thankfully, we will not rehash any of those arguments here. Philosophers may choose to grapple with this question, but believers seem to take a different, more practical approach to dealing with the existence of pain and suffering in God's world.

Anyone who knows a good many people with quality, long-term sobriety has certainly noticed a remarkable characteristic that all such people seem to have in common—an almost uncanny equanimity to life's ups and downs. Even more astounding is how opposite this is from the addict's nature, which, as we have mentioned, is abnormally irascible, moody, and hypersensitive. It seems that the recovering addict no longer searches in vain for an answer to the "Why do bad things happen?" question. Indeed, it seems that he or she has come to regard it as quite the nonquestion. The real question is, "Do bad things happen at all?" This is not a word game. This is an expression of humility and faith. Can I really say that something is bad because I don't like it?

*evenness of temps**

The Ba'al Shem Tov described this attitude of trust as the constant awareness of God's Presence. The Psalmist says (16:8), "I have set God before me at all times." The Ba'al Shem Tov relates the Hebrew word for "I have set"—*shivvisi*—with the word *shaveh*, meaning "equal," and explains that one who sets God before him is one for whom "no matter what, whether people praise you or shame you ... it is all 'equal' ... Whether you eat delicacies or other things, it is all 'equal' ... Whatever happens, you say, 'This too comes from God and must therefore be all right.'" The Ba'al Shem Tov then adds, "[But] this is a very high level." In assuming this attitude—that nothing that happens in one's life can truly be deemed bad— the recovering addict attains a rare level of acceptance and trust that most men and women seem to be able to live without. The addict, however, in order to live, is forced to utterly abandon the notion that if I don't like something, then it can't be good, and if it's good, then I am sure to like it.

In the Talmud, this sentiment is expressed by Rabbi Akiva's adage: "All that the Merciful does, He does for the good."

The Talmud relates a story in which Rabbi Akiva's attitude was put to the test. He was once traveling and came to a walled city, where he sought shelter, but the people of the city refused to let him in. Rabbi Akiva said, "All that the Merciful does, He does for the good," and went to sleep in a field outside of the city walls. He had been traveling with three items—a donkey, a rooster, and a lamp. Soon, a lion came and devoured his donkey. Rabbi Akiva said, "All that the Merciful does, He does for the good." A cat came and ate his rooster. Rabbi Akiva said, "All that the Merciful does, He does for the good." A wind came and blew out his lamp. Rabbi Akiva said, "All that the Merciful does, He does for the good." In the morning, he discovered that during the night, a band of marauders had come and attacked the city. Had he been allowed to sleep there, he would have met the same dismal fate as the others. Had the marauders heard his donkey bray or his rooster crow, he would have been spotted; certainly, if they had seen his lamp, they would have found him right away. Thus, all of the seemingly unfortunate events that happened that night saved Rabbi Akiva's life. Indeed, everything that happened was for the good.

The Talmud's message is that man, with his limited vision, cannot possibly see the true significance of earthly events. He must therefore withhold his subjective evaluation of things and accept the events of his life with the faith that God knows all, can do all, and is the essence of good.

The Ba'al Shem Tov taught that nothing happens in this world by chance. Rather, God carefully orchestrates every detail of His creation by means of *hashgachah peratis*—literally "individualized supervision" but more loosely translated as Divine Providence. "Even when the wind carries a fallen leaf from one place to another," said the Ba'al Shem Tov, "That, too, is *hashgachah peratis*." No detail of creation is left to chance.

I once heard an alcoholic state emphatically that his "H.P." was guiding every aspect of his life. I couldn't figure out how he knew about the concept of *hashgachah peratis*, let alone the Hebrew term for it. Later, it dawned on me that "H.P." meant "Higher Power." Even later it dawned on me that there really isn't any difference.

CHAPTER 9
FORBEARANCE

God's "Secret"

So, God is powerful, and God is kind. God can be trusted and relied upon to carry us through whatever vicissitudes life brings. However, all of this assumes that our relationship with Him is in proper order. What if we have severed or damaged our connection to God? Can it be repaired? Is God willing to give us a second chance?

Tolerance, acceptance, and forgiveness are indispensable to the survival of any intimate relationship—even more so in our relationship with God. We must know that we are never beyond redemption, that we are able to re-establish our bond with Him at any time, no matter what we have done to distance ourselves from Him in the past.

In Steps 5, 6, and 7, the recovering addict is guided through a process of removing the blockages that impede his or her connection to God. The very fact that this process is prescribed implies that God, for His part, is willing to restore the damaged relationship. These Steps make clear a presupposition that God is tolerant and forgiving. As the prophet Ezekiel (33:11) exhorted the people, "[God] takes no pleasure in the death of the wicked, but rather that they turn away from their ways and live."

This is another distinct theological stance. The fact that God is willing to have a relationship with imperfect beings is not an idea that should be taken for granted. To wit, it was only after Moses beseeched God to forgive the people for the seemingly unforgivable sin of the Golden Calf that God revealed to Moses the secret of the Thirteen Attributes of Mercy. God told Moses that whenever the people were in need of compassion, they could invoke His Attributes of Mercy by enumerating them as follows:

> God, compassionate and gracious, slow to anger, and abundant in kindness and truth; preserver of kindness for thousands of generations, forgiver of iniquity, willful sin, and error ... Who cleanses ... (Exodus 34:6-7)

The Talmud says, "Were this not an explicit verse, we could never have said such a thing on our own." In other words, if God Himself had not divulged this secret to Moses, we would have no reason to assume that God is willing to bear our imperfections or to reconcile with those who have transgressed His will.

In addition to the above-mentioned verses in Exodus, the Zohar points to another passage in Scripture that also contains Thirteen Attributes of Mercy. The "Superior Thirteen Attributes," as they are called, are found in the writings of the prophet Micah (7:18–20):

> Who is a God like You, who bears transgression, and pardons the wrong-doing of the remnant of His inheritance? He does not sustain His anger forever, for He desires loving kindness. He will, once more, have compassion on us; [and] forget our transgressions; and You will hurl all our sins into the depths of the ocean. Grant truth to Jacob, [and] loving kindness to Abraham, as You vowed to our forefathers long ago.

The sixteenth-century kabbalist Moses Cordovero elucidates the meaning of each of the attributes as follows:

1. "Who is a God like You"—God enlivens us even when we choose to misappropriate this vitality.
2. "Who bears transgression"—God protects us from being consumed by the negativity that we have unleashed, thus giving us the opportunity to return to Him.
3. "And pardons the wrongdoing"—When we return to Him, God cleanses us.
4. "Of the remnant of His heritage"—God empathizes with our pain, for we are His "inheritance."
5. "He does not sustain His anger forever"—God allows Himself to be appeased.
6. "For He desires loving kindness"—God lovingly emphasizes our merits, not our deficiencies.
7. "He will once more have compassion on us"—God grants a fresh start to those who return to Him.
8. "[And] forget our transgressions"—God chooses to "forget" our past misdeeds so that they do not interfere with our present relationship with Him.

9. "And You will hurl all our sins into the depths of the ocean"—God views our mistakes as expendable.
10. "Grant truth to Jacob"—God is kind even to those who only uphold the basic letter of the law, which is personified by Jacob.
11. "[And] loving kindness to Abraham"—God displays generosity, as did our forefather, Abraham.
12. "As You vowed to our forefathers"—God conveys merit upon us that is not our own but that of our ancestors.
13. "Long ago"—When not even the merit of our ancestors is sufficient, God remembers His original love for His people.

Forgiveness vs. Atonement

It is clear from the wording of Steps 5, 6, and 7 that their aim is not just to assist us in obtaining pardon or expiation of guilt. Their main purpose is to fully restore our relationship with God. Judaism calls this process *kaparah*, which means "cleansing" or "atonement" and is very different than plain forgiveness. As soon as a person mends his or her ways (and makes restitution when necessary), God immediately forgives. But that does not mean that the damage to the relationship has been repaired. If your teenaged son takes the car out without permission and gets into a fender-bender, you may not punish him if he is sufficiently contrite, but that does not mean that your full trust for him has been re-instated. Forgiveness just means the waiving of punishment, but atonement is complete reconciliation. Indeed, the origin of the English word atonement is "at-one-ment"—the state of being "at one"—again—with God.

What Steps 5, 6, and 7 indicate is that God makes Himself available for reconciliation. Just as we want to be "at one" with Him, He wants to be "at one" with us, and He is ready to accept us despite our past failings. This is unmistakably the sentiment that underlies the "Seventh Step Prayer":

"My Creator, I am now willing that you should have all of me, good and bad. I pray that You now remove from me every single defect of character which stands in the way of my usefulness to you and my fellows. Grant me strength, as I go out from here, to do your bidding. Amen." (*Alcoholics Anonymous*, p. 76)

Judaism teaches that God has no interest in using our failings against us to push us even further away from Him. He is not like a mortal of flesh and blood who holds a grudge, nor does He spurn us for being imperfect. To the contrary, God willingly accepts all those who return to Him. In the words of King David: ". . . a broken and a contrite heart, You God, will not despise" (Psalms 51:19).

A Dynamic Relationship

On the other hand, as the wording of the Seventh Step Prayer implies, although God is open to our advances should we turn to Him, He does not force us to do so. He waits for us to be ready and willing. When we do approach Him, He not only reciprocates, He also multiplies the effect of our efforts.

Our sages conveyed this thought in many ways:

God says, "My children, make for Me an opening the size of an eye of a needle, and I will make for you openings big enough for wagons and carriages to pass through."

One who comes to purify oneself is then granted ample assistance from on High.

One who sanctifies oneself even a small bit down in this world is then greatly sanctified from Heaven.

This also brings us to appreciate another aspect of our concept of God—His humility. Yes, God is humble. And what is humility but making space for another?

God makes the process of reunion and reconciliation conditional on our approaching Him. Rather than dominating us, God allows us to have an active and defining role in our relationship with Him. In the case of Steps 5, 6, and 7, we have to be truthful with Him about our faults (Step Five); we have to be ready to change (Step Six); and we have to ask for His help (Step Seven). In short, just as God grants us the freedom to stray from Him, He gives us the freedom to seek means of returning. In either case, He has given us room to make our own choice.

We might say that God has entered into a dynamic and collaborative relationship with His creations. He has actually made us partners with Him. There is a Chasidic interpretation of the verse (Genesis 1:26) "And God said, 'Let us make man . . .' " as God's call to each and every one of us. God says to each one of us, "Let's make a man." God invites the individual to be a partner in the process of his or her own development as a human being. This is key to our understanding of God. Many of us can admit that God must really be great, but we can't imagine that He would want to have a relationship with someone like us. Of course, this kind of sanctimonious despair is really just an excuse to leave God out of our lives. Sometimes we like to say that God is mean and intolerant so that we can give up on Him. That is why it is vital that we know that God does not give up on us.

When God created the world, He was not starting a business. He was entering into a relationship. We are not just God's employees; we are His children. A business needs to make a profit, and employees who don't pull their weight are let go. A family is different. A parent doesn't disown a child for "underperforming" or "failing to produce." Indeed, there is no such concept in a healthy and loving family. To the contrary, when a child strays—even the most vexing and troublesome child—no loving parent will say "good riddance." The parent waits for the child's return and experiences great pleasure when the child chooses to do so.

In other words, God has certain expectations for His children. He wants us to live good lives and to treat each other kindly. He wants us to be obedient to Him—but more than He wants any of those things, He wants us to be close to Him. God's greatest desire is not that His children behave perfectly but that they come back *home*. Hence, even when we have violated His will in other ways, His most intense desire remains His will for us to remain *connected* to Him. This brings us to the very important discussion of God's will.

CHAPTER 10
WILL

What God Wants

Of all the Steps, the Eleventh speaks most directly about our relationship with God and how that connection is maintained.

The step reads:

"Sought through prayer and meditation to improve our conscious contact with God as we understood Him, praying only for knowledge of His will for us and the power to carry that out."

More than just telling us how to *seek* God, this Step informs our *concept* of God like no other.

At first reading, it may be easy to miss, but with a little bit of thought, we can see that the Eleventh Step makes what is perhaps the most significant statement about God to be found in all of the Steps. There's an immensely important word in this Step—the word *will*. Let's read the Step again with added emphasis:

"Sought through prayer and meditation to improve our conscious contact with God as we understood Him, praying only for knowledge of His *will* for us and the power to carry that out."

God has a will.

This is an incredibly important point.

Step Three, which speaks of God's caring as well as Steps Five, Six, and Seven, which allude to His desire for a relationship with us, both imply that God has a will. He *wants* to care for us. He *wants* to have a relationship with us (indeed, even more than He *wants* us to behave perfectly). But here, in Step Eleven, God's will is explicitly mentioned for the first time. And not only does He have a will, He also has a *specific* "will for *us*." God *wants* something from the individual.

Need vs. Want

Many philosophical and religious systems view the idea of God's wanting something as problematic. How can an infinite and perfect being want, or be in want of, anything? Does this not imply a lacking of something or someone?

Judaism, however, is not at all troubled by this concept. Indeed, the very foundation of Judaism as a *covenantal* religion is that God most certainly *does* want something from us. God promises to uphold His end of the deal, but He asks for certain things in return. As God told Abraham, father of the Jewish people:

"I will establish My covenant as an everlasting covenant . . .As for you, you must keep My covenant, you, and your descendants after you for the generations to come" (Genesis 17:7-9).

Again, just prior to the Revelation at Sinai, God tells Moses:

"Now if you obey Me fully and keep My covenant, then out of all nations you will be my treasured possession . . . " (Exodus 19:5).

God is clearly asking for something. The particular aspects of His will—what He wants and does not want—are the very basis of Torah law. The commandments are not technical rules but an expression of God's desires. Indeed, as the kabbalists describe it, God made Himself vulnerable, so-to-speak, by articulating His likes and dislikes and allowing His creations free choice of whether or not to abide by these wishes. This is how God makes Himself available for intimacy with His creations. As such, Judaism does not view adherence to God's commandments so much as a matter of obedience as a matter of sensitivity to God's desire. That is not to say that without our compliance, God is somehow incomplete. God requires nothing. He has no needs. But He does have a will—a will to be in a relationship with us.

In fact, this will is no less than the driving force behind all of creation.

Because God needs nothing, He also did not need to create. Had He chosen not to be a Creator, He would still be God. Yet God *wants* to create. And He *wants* to create because He *wants* something from His creations. In the words of the Midrash, God made the world because "He *yearned* to have a dwelling place in the lower realms." The Chasidic masters explain this to mean that God created the world because of a passionate desire to be "at home" in a realm inhabited by sentient beings with free will and ego-consciousness. Why God wants this, well, we cannot know. Indeed, the very difference between a *need* and a *desire* is that a need can be "rationally" defended but a desire has no "practical" explanation. As Rabbi Schneur Zalman, founder of the Chabad school of Chasidism, used to say when discussing the nature of God's will for creation, "When it comes to a desire, you cannot ask rational questions."

For example, let's say your spouse says that they *need* something; it is possible to ask them to explain their need. If they cannot, you might even be able to argue that they don't really need it. However, if your spouse says that they *want* something, even if they cannot convincingly explain why, it doesn't mean that they don't really want it. That's the *definition* of a want as opposed to a need. A need is practical. A desire is impractical. Thus, the appropriate response to a desire is either to fulfill it or not to fulfill it, but not to argue with it. So, too, when we speak of God's will, we mean His irrational, impractical desire. The very impracticality of God's relationship with us is what makes it intimate as opposed to utilitarian. God doesn't need us. He *wants* us.

The Intimacy of Will

I was once teaching this subject in a Torah class. One woman, a very intelligent and no-nonsense type lady, had a major problem with the concept that God would want anything from people. She kept saying that it didn't make any sense. I told her that that was exactly right; it didn't make any sense. But she kept struggling with the idea because she wanted to understand our relationship with God in practical terms. But our relationship with God is not practical. It is wonderfully impractical, and that is precisely what makes it so intimate.

"I know you to be a competent and responsible adult," I said to her, "and I am certain that if you wanted flowers on your wedding anniversary that you would have no problem finding them, paying for them, and bringing them home all by yourself. You could even write yourself a note to attach to them. So, tell me, why do you want your husband to do something for you that you are perfectly capable of doing yourself?" She immediately understood the point. One cannot understand God's relationship with His creations from a cold and analytical perspective, because God's relationship with us is not rational. It's not about practicality. It's about desire, and desire is not rational. It is not subintelligent but supraintelligent; it transcends logic. After all, that is what every good romance is about—a commitment that transcends logic. In this romance, God reveals to us His very irrational desire for us to be close to Him. And as in any romance, the most meaningful and intimate bond is forged through the fulfillment of irrational desire. We are free to choose whether or not to comply with God's will for us, but we don't ask God to prove that His will is valid. It is as valid as He is.

This is the amazing thing about desire. Desire transcends all else. Desire is the window to vulnerability, bonding, and intimacy. The fact that God has a will for us and shares that will with us means that He has made Himself available to us to connect to Him in the most meaningful way.

The Opportunity to Connect

As we mentioned earlier, God expresses His will by giving us a commandment. The Hebrew word "mitzvah" is often colloquially used to mean a good deed; more plainly translated, it means a "commandment." However, the word mitzvah means so much more: it comes from the word *tzavsah*, which means "connection." A mitzvah is a connection, or an opportunity to connect. The fulfillment of will connects us where intellect falls short. In other words, it is *action* more than feelings, more than understanding, and more than faith that actually connects us to God. This is a quintessentially Jewish concept.

At Sinai when Moses asked the people if they were ready to accept God's commandments, they responded, "We will do, and we will understand" (Exodus 24:7). If we wanted to understand and then do, we would likely never understand and we would certainly never do. By doing, even without understanding, we connect to God and ultimately, also come to understand Him to the extent that we can. We cannot intellectualize our way into a meaningful relationship with God. Our finite minds cannot grasp Him. But we can become wonderfully united with Him through the fulfillment of His will, and for that, there is no mental prerequisite.

To state it bluntly, just having a "God of our understanding" is not enough for us—even if we understand our God to be powerful, caring, forgiving, and all of the other qualities we have previously discussed. We must also know that God has a will so that despite our limited understanding of Him we can always connect to Him through simple action.

Remember the woman whom I asked why she didn't buy herself flowers on her anniversary? There is an epilogue to that story. As it turns out, this woman had a hard time expressing her desires to her husband. She didn't actually send herself flowers, but pretty close. She felt that she was being responsible and self-sufficient by taking care of herself. At the same time, she felt disappointed that her husband failed to read her mind and do the things for her that she wanted. Some time after our discussion, her husband approached me and thanked me for improving their marriage. He said that he had been frustrated that he did not know how to connect to his wife. This changed when she started sharing with him her wants and desires, even regarding things that she would have normally taken care of herself. Essentially, she hadn't realized that by failing to express her will, she was actually depriving her husband of the opportunity to connect to her.

By having a will for us, God lets us be connected to Him. He invites us to become an extension of His will. In so doing, He gives us a gift. He allows us to be of significance. He tells us that we matter to Him in the most profound way.

The Opportunity to Transcend

As we have already mentioned many times, albeit in a variety of words, the addict's basic problem is an obsession with self. In order to live happily and usefully, the addict needs a way to transcend his or her own ego. But how does one get outside of oneself? Our answer is that one transcends self by connecting to the Infinite. But this then begs the question—exactly how does one connect to the Infinite?

As we have just explained, one connects through the fulfillment of a will. Not the exertion of self-will, but the surrender of it in deference to the will of God.

Many NA meetings close with that fellowship's "Third Step Prayer":

"Take my will and my life. Guide me in my recovery. Show me how to live" (*Narcotics Anonymous*, 6th ed., p. 26).

In other words, the Steps talk about a God who has a specific will for us, a God who asks for things, and who allows Himself to be served, because a God who wants nothing, who has no opinion, or preferences cannot be served. And without the opportunity to serve, one cannot transcend the self—and one cannot recover.

Good Orderly Direction

In the original draft of the Big Book submitted to the early members of the fellowship for review, the Third Step read, "Made a decision to turn our will and our lives over to the care *and direction* of God . . ." After some debate, the word *direction* was deleted because it was considered overbearing. The basic idea, however, has remained a cornerstone of the program. A working concept of God as outlined in Twelve-Step programs includes the idea that God gives us direction. As many in recovery are wont to say, God is an acronym for Good Orderly Direction.

It is interesting to consider that the Zohar says: "God and the Torah are entirely one." The Zohar also says that the word Torah comes from the word *hora'ah*—"direction" or "instruction." Therefore, essentially, direction from God is another way of referring to God. When we have God's instruction in life, we have God in our life.

His Will, Not Mine

As noted above in reference to Step Two, the problem of the addict is primarily an obsession with control. This is why it is so important to see God as a "power greater than ourselves," so that one may feel free to actually surrender control. However, in order to address fully the issue of control, it must be recognized that the addict's desire for control is just that—a desire. In other words, the addict has a will. He or she *wants* to be in control. Recovery means realizing that God *also* has a will—and then *deciding* to place that will before one's own.

Describing the Eleventh Step's call for regular prayer and meditation, the Big Book says: "We usually conclude the period of meditation with a prayer that we be shown all through the day what our next step is to be

...We ask especially for freedom from self-will ..." (p. 87).

We Jews have a prayer in our early morning liturgy that states:

> May it be Your will, Lord my God and God of our fathers, to accustom us
> to following Your instructions, and to adhere to the fulfillment of Your
> commandments.... Let not our evil inclination have mastery over us; ...
> [rather] force our inclination to be subservient to You.

God has a will; each of us has a will. Being connected to God is about making ourselves more concerned with what He wants than what we want. As the Mishnah says: "Make His will your own will."

The Lubavitcher Rebbe explained this teaching to mean that although the strict letter of the law requires us to fulfill God's will whether we like it or not, the sages encourage us to go beyond mere observance of the law and actually remake our will to be aligned to God's. Fulfilling God's will should not be a burden but a manifestation of our truest self. When a person can undergo such a change, something incredible begins to happen. As the Mishnah continues, "And He will then fulfill your will as if it were His will." God will lead the person into the circumstances most conducive to expressing his or her desire to do God's will.

Most old-timers in recovery will attest to the fact that when one lives to do God's will, not only does one's attitude improve, but somehow, somewhat inexplicably, life actually gets better as well. I have heard this sentiment expressed succinctly many times by many people in recovery. "I tried my way. My way doesn't work. I tried His way. His way works."

The phrase "Thy will be done" is found three times in the Big Book. The wording is obviously a direct reference to the Lord's Prayer of the Christian liturgy. But an interesting emendation is made to these words on p. 85, where it states, in relation to the Eleventh Step: "Every day is a day when we must carry the vision of God's will into all of our activities. 'How can I best serve Thee—Thy will (not mine) be done.'"

The context of the phrase and the notable insertion of the words "not mine" in parentheses put quite a new spin on these words, not to be found in the original. Here, "Thy will be done" is used as a request to God that in all areas of life, His will should overrule our own. In other words, the program is describing a God who has an opinion about "all of our activities." Whether we eat, sleep, do business, or pray, there is a way to do it that conforms to God's will. As King Solomon said: "In all your ways you should know Him, and He will make your paths straight" (Proverbs 3:6), or in the words of the Mishnah: "All your deeds should be for the sake of Heaven."

"Knowledge of His Will for Us"

We're about to conclude our discussion of will, but there remains an important idea that must be addressed. There are those who concede that God may have a will but think it arrogant to assume that we could ever hope to know what it is. Of course, Judaism is based on the idea that God has explicitly revealed His will and told His people exactly what He wants. This is precisely what occurred at the Revelation at Sinai more than three millennia and three centuries ago. Some may still argue that this constitutes only a general will but that God does not communicate a specific will for the individual.

In answer:

First, the commandments *are* a specific will for the individual. One cannot perform all of the commandments in every place and at every time. We fulfill the commandments wherever and whenever they are applicable to the situation. Thus, by leading the individual to a particular situation where a specific commandment may be observed, God is certainly indicating His will for that person.

I once dealt with a young Jewish man who was suffering from mental illness. It was time for a group meeting, and he was nowhere to be found, so I went to the dormitory to fetch him. I found him collapsed in his bed. I asked him whether he was able to get up. He replied that he was able but that he did not want to. I asked him why not. He told me that he did not want to move until God told him to do so. I went to the library and brought back a copy of the *Concise Code of Jewish Law* from which I then read to him: "When one awakens in the morning, one must immediately recognize and appreciate the kindness God has done with him ... One should say [the prayer *I give thanks*] ... and by doing so, he will realize that God is in his midst and will immediately get out of bed and prepare himself for the service of God." The young man thought about these words and got out of bed.

Second, if we are to believe in God's meticulous Providence for every detail in His creation, then we also believe that God will show us the right path in every aspect of life. This does not have to come in the form of prophecy or a booming voice from the clouds. God's will can be revealed to us in a number of ways that are perfectly natural and normal. As the Ba'al Shem Tov taught: "Everything a person sees or hears can be taken as a lesson in serving the Creator." In the words of the Big Book , "God will constantly disclose more to you and to us . . . The answers will come, if your own house is in order" (p. 164).

"And the Power to Carry that Out"

By deferring his or her own personal will, the recovering addict inevitably finds a new way of living that is infinitely more fulfilling than a life of active addiction. Yet there are still those who are uncomfortable with the notion of such complete surrender. They think it a prescription for passivity.

The Jewish view, however, is that submission to God's will is the key to effective living. With self-will, one is limited to drawing upon one's own finite ability and wherewithal. Eventually, one is bound to confront an obstacle or an impasse that cannot be negotiated or overcome. By doing things "God's way" rather than our own, we channel the force of the Creator. And nothing can stop the force of the Creator in His creation.

Thus, we return to our first concept of God that we gleaned from the Steps—that He is Power. Giving up on self-will in order to do God's will is not passivity. It does not mean that one has no will. It means that one's will now comes from a higher place than his or her own needs and wants. Indeed, Judaism sees this as the ultimate level of human existence. For this reason, the patriarchs—Abraham, Isaac, and Jacob—are lauded as being "chariots" of the Divine Will, meaning that they lived their entire lives in a state of complete surrender to God. As Chasidus teaches, even the average person attains the same quality of self-nullity whenever he or she fulfills any of the commandments. One actually becomes a conduit, at that moment, to channel the Divine. In other words, whenever one submits to the will of God, one automatically receives "the power to carry that out."

We give God our will, and God gives us His power.

PART IV
HEALING EACH OTHER

The sages teach: "Make for yourself a teacher; acquire for yourself a friend; and judge every person favorably." Sponsorship, fellowship, and tolerance as keys to recovery.

CHAPTER 11
SPONSORSHIP

Return to Humanity . . . and Reality

I once heard an addict humorously relate, "I can't stand other people. That's why it's ironic that I care so much what they think of me."

Recovery, as a process of spiritual growth, demands not only that we heal our relationships with others but more so, that we realize that *it is through our relationships with others* that *we are healed.*

Many in recovery are wont to point out that the first word in the Steps is "we" and that recovery, as such, is a "we program." They will also tell you that the difference between the "well" and the "ill" is *we* and *I.*

Addiction is fundamentally a disease of isolation. Through active addiction, one becomes wrapped up in self and increasingly divorced from everything that is objectively real. By developing the appropriate positive relationships with others, the addict is gradually released from the prison of self-obsession.

Primarily, the Twelve Steps prescribe a relationship with God as the means for transcending the ego. However, it is impossible to keep this relationship separate from our dealings with other human beings. As the Chasidic masters taught, "If one loves the Father, one must love all His children." To be sure, there are various kinds of relationships that are needed for our well-being. Not all relationships are the same, nor do they need to be, but all are indispensable. All get us out of ourselves and connect us with Reality.

Three Kinds of Relationships

The sages teach in the Mishnah: "Make for yourself a teacher; acquire for yourself a friend; and judge each person favorably."

If we look closely, we will notice that the sages are enumerating three specific components to our connectedness with others. To state each one in a word, they are: Mentorship ("Make for yourself a teacher"), fellowship ("acquire for yourself a friend"), and tolerance ("and judge every person favorably.")

Instructions of the Sages	Ideal Described
"Make for yourself a teacher"	Mentorship
"Acquire for yourself a friend"	Fellowship
"Judge every person favorably"	Tolerance

Not surprisingly, in recovery as well we find that these three virtues are stressed as vital elements of healing and growth. Those in recovery find it crucial to have a mentor, someone to check in with and to look to for guidance. Having a sponsor is considered as essential as any other ingredient of working a successful Twelve-Step program. Fellowship is another cornerstone of recovery. The entire premise of Twelve-Step groups is that people who share a common problem can recover together and that their mutual understanding and support provides that which no amount of outside professional help can replace. Finally, the Twelve Steps teach that we must have compassion and understanding for all. The addict in recovery learns that it is necessary to be at peace with all people, and that negative attitudes toward others, such as resentment, intolerance, and indignation, only serve to keep us sick.

The Lubavitcher Rebbe explained that these three principles are presented in conjunction with one another to serve as an all-inclusive instruction of how to address the totality of the human race. Among people, we will find those in whom we recognize some superior quality, those whom we admire and would like to emulate. Then there are those whom we may not necessarily look to as mentors, but with whom we share certain like-mindedness or a common goal. Finally, there are those people with whom we see no reason to associate. We cannot look up to them nor can we even relate to them as peers. They may be individuals who are seriously flawed, those who have hurt us, or even people who are truly unhealthy for us to be around. But even these people are still to be judged favorably. We are by nature exceedingly skilled at finding justifications for ourselves and, at the same time, being judgmental of others. In truth, however, we should save our piercing scrutiny for ourselves and use our great powers of rationalizing to see others in a positive light.

In this chapter, we shall discuss the first of these three aspects of interpersonal relationships—how we relate to those whom we recognize as being above us. Then, in the chapters that follow, we will discuss in detail the other kinds of relationships as well.

Free Yourself of Doubt

It's interesting to me that people who know little else about recovery have somehow heard about the idea of a sponsor. But what is a sponsor?

What a sponsor is *not* is someone who will take care of your problems for you. I have heard many sponsors tell new sponsees, "I'm not your lawyer or your bank. Do not call me to get you out of jail or for a loan."

So what is a sponsor? Some old-timers sum it all up with a cute acronym—S.P.O.N.S.O.R. is "Sane Person Offering Newcomers Suggestions On Recovery."

More specifically, a sponsor is a mentor; a sponsor is someone to whom to be accountable; a sponsor is someone whom you trust because they possess the qualities that you would like to have yourself.

Interestingly enough, if this is our definition of sponsor, then according to the Torah, everybody should have a sponsor.

In addition to the above-quoted teaching from the Mishnah, the very same words are repeated again by another sage in another teaching. "Make for yourself a teacher and free yourself of doubt. Do not tithe by estimation, even if giving in excess of the required amount." The question is asked, since the directive to have a teacher was already mentioned (earlier in the very same chapter of the same volume, no less), why was it found necessary to restate it here?

In this second version of the teaching, a reason is given for the importance of having a mentor—". . . free yourself of doubt." Without someone to look to for guidance, one can become mired in uncertainty. The role of a mentor is to help clarify those matters you find perplexing so that you can make a decision one way or the other without hesitation or regret. The sponsor may offer clarity in a number of ways, including sharing lessons learned from personal experiences, directing the sponsee to review program literature, or encouraging the sponsee to seek the advice of others in the fellowship.

Further, the context of this teaching is important. It juxtaposes the two statements "Make for yourself a teacher . . ." and "Do not tithe by estimation . . ." If one is uncertain of one's obligations, he or she might decide to act more stringently than necessary, as in the case of one who does not know how to measure how much to give to charity and thus gives an overly liberal amount. The Mishnah tells us that this is not a desirable approach. Very often, the best of intentions leads one to overextend oneself, creating an untenable situation. It may seem preferable to err on the side of caution and do more than one is obligated, yet ultimately, such a plan is doomed to fail. One should instead find a teacher who can give him or her clear guidelines as to the exact nature of his or her obligations and then follow that teacher's advice, whether it seems to be lenient or stringent.

In working a Twelve-Step program, one of the vital functions of a sponsor is to provide clarity. I once knew a fellow in recovery named Fred. Fred was already in the program for a few years and was on Step Ten—"Continued to take personal inventory and when we were wrong, promptly admitted it." In his zeal to work the Step properly he had forced himself to develop a habit of immediately apologizing to anyone whom he thought that he had offended or wronged. The problem was that since taking this Step, his relationships with others had gotten worse—at home, at work, with friends. Instead of smoothing things over, he was getting into confrontations. Fred finally spoke to his sponsor and explained his dilemma. He was truly baffled, for after all, he was only doing what the program advised. His sponsor only had to listen to a few examples of how Fred's Tenth Step was getting him into trouble before giving him the following advice: "The Step says we *take inventory*, and when we're wrong we promptly admit it. How fast can you possibly take inventory?" Fred's sponsor's advice to him was to take just one inventory at the end of the day before bed, and if he found himself at fault in any way, he could talk to the people concerned the next day.

The most important point to be made is that the advice of Fred's sponsor is in no way universal. Not everyone has to work the Step that way. For some people, they might actually need to make amends as quickly as possible. The point is that by talking to a sponsor, Fred gained a certain clarity that he may not have come to on his own. This leads us to yet another point.

A New Perspective

Another important aspect of sponsorship is that it allows one to assume a perspective different from one's own. The value of being able to "get out of your own head" cannot be underestimated. When one is stuck in his or her own way of perceiving things, there can often seem to be nowhere to turn. A sponsor has the distinct advantage of being someone who is not you and sees your life from a different, usually far more objective, vantage point.

There's an AA saying that even when you give up alcohol, you still have alcohol*ism*. What is "ism"? "I Sponsor Myself." In other words, physical sobriety is easy to achieve. Gaining an outlook on life that is drastically different from the one that you're used to is much harder.

The Torah says that when Moses beheld the burning bush, he remarked, "Let me move away from here, and see this great sight ..." (Exodus 3:3). Literally, this means what it sounds like. Moses physically moved from the place where he had been standing in order to gain a better view of the bush. On a deeper level, the Ba'al Shem Tov explained that the verse describes a shift in spiritual perspective as well. If one wishes to behold the divine, he must be ready to move from his current stance and assume a new way of looking at things. Thus, upon encountering the divine, even a righteous and highly refined individual such as Moses saw fit to move to a new vantage point.

The Talmud says, "A person is always biased toward himself." Thus, we must always "move away from here"—from the inherent subjectivity of where we presently stand and try to gain a new perspective. In other words, we learn not to rely solely on our own view.

The Ba'al Shem Tov explains further that God's decision to reveal Himself to Moses in a thorn bush is also significant. God could have chosen a more majestic tree, but He desired to show Himself to Moses in the midst of a scraggly shrub, as if to say that a lofty ego cannot serve as a resting place for the Divine. Our pride tells us that we should be able to dictate terms on which God is to come to us; that He should meet us where we stand. But, in truth, no matter how far along in our spiritual development we may be, it is only by letting go of old prejudices and preconceived notions that we allow ourselves to be receptive to God.

Now, one might ask, is a sponsor infallible, so that one may equate listening to one's sponsor to listening to God? The answer, quite obviously, is that a sponsor is not a prophet, nor is he or she incapable of poor judgment. A sponsor is not appointed by God. A sponsor is much greater than that. A sponsor is appointed by *you*!

The power of the sponsor comes from the person who agrees to take the sponsor's advice. God can communicate with us in all sorts of ways. There is nothing marvelous in that. What is of the utmost significance, however, is that when we allow ourselves the possibility of stepping away from our own viewpoint and open ourselves up to taking direction from someone else, we remove the greatest, nay, the *only* impediment to conscious contact with God there is. That great impediment is ego, and whenever the ego is quieted, we are always more receptive to truth.

"Make for Yourself a Teacher"

Now, let's look again more closely at the words of the Mishnah. "Make for yourself a teacher." The wording seems a bit odd. What does it mean to "make" a teacher? And what does it mean to make a teacher "for yourself." We could have translated the Mishnah in a way that would have read more smoothly in English—"Provide a teacher for yourself," or something of the like—but then we would lose out on some important nuances of the teaching.

One meaning of "making" a teacher is that one must do just that—one must "make" someone *become* a teacher. Being a sponsor is not an intrinsic status. A sponsor is not a sponsor without a sponsee. In other words, you are the one who makes your sponsor a sponsor. You invest in him or her the power to guide you. This is an incredibly important idea. Agreeing to take direction from someone does not make us weak. To the contrary, it is one of the more powerful decisions that are ours to make.

When we cannot bring ourselves to receive guidance, that is when we are weak, because it means that we cannot break out of personal limitations. This brings us to another nuance of the wording "make for yourself a teacher." Even if you don't feel like it, you must gather your strength and make yourself have a teacher.

There is yet another reading of these words. One does not attend classes or undergo a certification process to become a sponsor. True, a sponsor may take some guidance from his or her own sponsor, but one really becomes a sponsor only through the experience of being one. In that process, the feedback from the sponsee is fundamental. The sponsee can help to "make" a teacher by honestly telling the sponsor how he or she is doing. The sponsor and sponsee are partners in a relationship, and the sponsee has an obligation to make that relationship work, just as the sponsor has that obligation. As the Mishnah says: "Much have I learned from my teachers, even more from my colleagues, and from my students most of all."

The Golden Sponsor

Rosie was a woman who just couldn't seem to get it together. She had been in recovery for several years and yet she wasn't staying sober and her life continued to get increasingly unmanageable. One day, Rosie was complaining to me that she didn't think that the program was for her. She said that her problem was her current living situation. She had been sharing an apartment with a woman who was out of work and didn't pay rent. But Rosie said that she couldn't get rid of the roommate because she, Rosie, was the one who had crashed her roommate's car, which made it "impossible" for her roommate to get to work and which was what led to her losing her job. Please don't laugh or roll your eyes. This was Rosie's situation, or at least how she understood her situation to be, and as far as she could see it, she had no other choice but to move to a new city. She insisted that if she relocated, her life would change for the better; she asked me what I thought. Not wanting to become entangled in this mess, I simply asked her whether she had spoken to her sponsor. "Yeah, of course I spoke to my sponsor. She's the roommate I'm trying to get rid of."

One of the most misunderstood events in the Bible has to be the sin of the Golden Calf. Taken at face value, it is difficult to comprehend how the same people who had witnessed the miracles of the Exodus and the Revelation at Sinai could be led to worship a molten image of a calf. However, a deeper understanding of the episode reveals that the people did not intend to replace God with the Golden Calf. What they were looking for was a substitute for their leader, Moses. As the Torah states, the debacle only began "When the people saw that Moses was late in coming down from the mountain . . ." (Exodus 32:1).

Moses, a human being of flesh and blood, represented the people's tangible connection to God. As Moses related, "I was standing between God and you at the time [of the Revelation at Sinai]" (Deuteronomy 5:5). Although it was God who redeemed the people from Egypt and gave them the Commandments at Sinai, Moses served as the visible medium through which God brought about these wonders. Without Moses to facilitate their relationship with God, the people panicked and sought to replace him.

Tradition relates various reasons why the likeness of a calf was selected for this purpose, but one explanation, that of Rabbi Samson Raphael Hirsch, is that the people were interested in having a connection to God that they could make into their own beast of burden. The image of a domesticated animal symbolized an intermediary with God that could be manipulated and controlled. Moses made demands of the people; when necessary he rebuked them. A docile calf would do no such thing.

If we apply this teaching to our own lives, we may understand it as a warning against the dangers of ostensibly seeking spiritual guidance while actually trying to have our own way. Having a sponsor means being willing to take direction, not give it. It is true that in many circumstances the team of sponsor–sponsee has worked together to find a solution to a given problem, but at the end of the day, the sponsee must be willing to accept the sponsor's advice.

Whether a sponsor is always right or not is entirely beside the point. What is relevant is that when we get out of our own heads long enough to truly listen to someone else, we may also be able to hear God.

Make Yourself a Teacher

Our final point on the idea of sponsorship coincides with another interpretation of the teaching "Make for yourself a teacher." In the Hebrew, these words can just as easily be read, "Make yourself into a teacher." The ultimate in mentorship is when the student becomes a mentor to others. I once saw a bumper sticker that read, "Sponsors: Get one. Use one. Be one."

Twelve-Step groups are not hierarchies. There is no concept of initiation, matriculation, or rank. To wit, they say, "Be nice to newcomers. They may some day be your sponsor." Anyone can aspire to become a sponsor, and indeed, is encouraged to do so, for the benefits of giving are ultimately greater than those of receiving. As the Talmud says about giving charity, "More than the rich man does for the poor man, does the poor man do for the rich man." As a Chasidic saying tells us, by working with others, our own minds and hearts become refined and more receptive to Godliness a thousandfold.

CHAPTER 12
FELLOWSHIP

"Making" and "Acquiring"

Let's now take a closer look at the second teaching from the Mishnah that we first introduced at the beginning of this section: "Acquire for yourself a friend." (See Table on p. 92.)

The first question we may ask is why it says "*make* for yourself a teacher" but "*acquire* for yourself a friend." Rabbi Menachem Meiri, the thirteenth-century Spanish talmudist, explains that much more work is entailed in making something new than in merely acquiring something that already exists. This means, as we explained above, that we have to make someone be our teacher; we must empower a person to be our mentor and guide. A friend, on the other hand, is not someone who has to be groomed for the position. A friend is simply one to whom we can readily relate on an equal plane. A friend is already a friend. We need only connect to a friend as he or she is. Indeed, that may be the best definition of a friend: *someone to whom we can relate without any special work involved.*

Thus, in the most basic terms, friendship is based on *identification.* A friend is, quite simply, someone with whom we can *identify*. Fulfilling our need to find people with whom we readily identify can be essential to life itself. There is a talmudic adage that rhymes in the original Aramaic—"*O chavrusa, o misusa*," which literally means, "There is either friendship or there is death."

The expression comes from a story about a great sage who returned to his hometown after many decades and found his grandchildren and the grandchildren of his peers engaged in study. He joined them, identified himself, and tried to share his wisdom with them, but they could not relate to him. At that point, he became exceedingly pained and cried out the now famous words, "There is either friendship or there is death." The Jewish worldview is one that embraces life and does not use such morbid expressions lightly. Thus the Talmud is not merely stating a preference—

that a person would rather die than live without friends. The Talmud is stating a fact: One *cannot* live without friends.

The Need for Identification

On May 12, 1935, the Twelve-Step movement was born when an alcoholic New York stockbroker who had been sober for just three months was visiting Akron, Ohio, on business. For the past three months, the stockbroker had managed to keep sober only by busying himself with helping other drunks. He knew that the secret to sobriety was working with others. Now, away from home and with no one to help, he felt close to another drink. In the lobby of the hotel where he was staying, he paced back and forth between the cocktail lounge and the phone booth. At last, the phone booth won. The visitor from New York started calling clergymen out of the hotel directory and asking whether anyone knew an alcoholic to whom he could speak. Eventually, he was directed to an alcoholic physician whose wife had been trying to help him quit drinking. The two met, the stockbroker's urge to drink subsided, and the fellowship of AA was founded.

The New York stockbroker is better known to us as Bill W., the first AA, and the Akron physician as Dr. Bob, AA's cofounder. As Dr. Bob later recalled, what intrigued him about Bill and quickly won his confidence in him was that Bill was not trying to talk to Dr. Bob about the doctor's drinking but about his own. Bill spoke about himself and his personal experiences. It was the power of *identification* that forged the bond between the two men and began the fellowship of AA and all of the Twelve-Step groups that would come after it.

Ask the Sick

There is an old Yiddish saying, "Don't ask the doctor; ask the sick person." The very premise of the Twelve-Step fellowships is that people who share a common malady can help one another in a way that no one else can. Twelve-Step groups are not run by professionals or specially trained leaders who guide the therapeutic process. Indeed, there is nothing at all like a formal process. A meeting of a Twelve-Step group is by definition nothing more than two or more people with the same basic problem who come together to discuss a common solution. No one is an authority. No one is in charge. In this unique approach to healing, the clinician's role is conspicuously absent, and there is a profound sense of equality and interconnectedness rarely found even in groups intentionally assembled with group chemistry in mind. Even the sponsor, who is vested with some semblance of authority, is just another addict.

Some would suspect that such lack of structure would lead to chaos or, at the very least, a plethora of bad advice. Detractors are quick to invoke terms such as "the blind leading the blind" or "the inmates running the asylum." Yet, the experience of countless thousands of people the world over has shown that regular people can successfully help one another when frustrated clinicians and professionals have already tried and failed.

There are several reasons that peer help can be uniquely effective even when other methods have fallen short. To highlight a few of them, let's return to the story of the original cofounders of AA.

Realizing that the key to maintaining sobriety was working with others, the doctor told his new friend, "If you and I are going to stay sober, we had better get busy" (*Alcoholics Anonymous*, p. 188). They went down to the local hospital and found an alcoholic lawyer in the detox. The lawyer, Bill D., who was to become AA number 3, would recall years later that when he first heard that the two men had come to talk to him about alcoholism and that it was his wife who had allowed them in: "I resented this very much, until she informed me that they were a couple of drunks just as I was. That wasn't so bad, to tell it to another drunk" (*Ibid.*, pp. 184-185).

One of the most obvious benefits of fellowship is its disarming quality. Whereas people can be reticent to speak to a professional, they are apt to open up to someone whom they consider an equal.

Bill D.'s account continues:

> She told me that these two drunks she had been talking to had a plan whereby they thought they could quit drinking, and part of that plan was that they tell it to another drunk. This was going to help them stay sober. All the other people that had talked to me wanted to help *me* ... but I felt as if I would be a real stinker if I did not listen to a couple of fellows for a short time, if that would cure *them*. (*Ibid.*, p. 185)

Another important aspect of fellowship is the sense of duty that it evokes. Pride can often be an obstacle to getting help. But when one feels that others need him, it removes much of what the ego perceives as a threat.

Bill W. and Dr. Bob returned to see Bill D. for several days. On their final visit before Bill D. was released from the hospital, Bill W. and Dr. Bob found Bill D.'s wife, Henrietta, sitting with him by his bedside. As soon as they entered, Bill D. shot up, pointed at them with great excitement, and cried out, "These are the fellows I told you about. They are the ones who understand" (*Ibid.*, p. 189).

Ultimately, the most valuable currency that a friend can offer is that of *understanding*. The feeling that one is understood by others fosters a profound sense of hope and trust that nothing else can replace.

You Are Not Different

One of the points that we have mentioned enough times throughout this book so as to constitute a major theme is the addict's tendency to feel different. It is typical of addicts to go through life with a constant, nagging sense that somehow they are not like other people. At first, the addictive behavior seems to provide a most welcome sense of comfort and confidence that allows the addict to feel that he or she can deal with other people. Ultimately, the addiction becomes an all-consuming obsession, and the addict is left feeling—and actually being—more isolated than ever before. This feeling of uniqueness can be one of the greatest obstacles to recovery. "If you had my troubles, you would also need to ..." "How can you tell me my that my behaviors are abnormal? Abnormal for whom?" "You just don't understand; *that's* the problem."

How is one to break through to someone who feels positively misunderstood by everyone else in the world? It is in addressing this quandary that we come to realize another invaluable asset of the group. Not only does identification allow the addict to feel safe in recovery, but also, and more important, identification is a key element of recovery itself. Addiction is a disease of self-obsession. Recovery is healing through relating to God and to other human beings as a way of getting outside of the self.

God and the Group

Of course, Twelve-Step fellowships are not just about connecting to other people. Recovery through the Steps is about developing a relationship with God. Yet, these are not two separate things. One of the most powerful ways by which we connect with God is through our relationships with other people.

Jews are no strangers to the idea of people's getting closer to God by getting closer to one another. We see that in all aspects of Judaism, communal involvement plays a central role in our relationship with God.

Torah study most typically takes places in pairs or in groups. Indeed, the Mishnah says that "close association with fellows" is one of the forty-eight "methods by which Torah knowledge is acquired." This may seem odd, because Torah is Godly revelation. Presumably, one can either receive Godly revelation in one of two ways—either by being a prophet oneself, or having access to the teachings of a prophet. Yet, we are told that by relating closely with others, one actually acquires Torah. We learn from God by learning from each other!

When Jews pray, they endeavor to pray with a *minyan*, a quorum of ten, and we are told that the Divine Presence rests upon every quorum, regardless of who the individuals are who make up the group. The Talmud relates that a heretic once chided one of the sages by saying, "You say that upon each and every quorum, the Divine Presence rests. So tell me, how many "Divine Presences" have you then?" To which the sage responded—in typical rabbinical fashion—with another question, "Does the sun shine in your house as well?" Just as the sun enters through countless windows into countless homes across the face of the earth, so does each group act like another window through which God's Presence shines.

Studying Torah and praying in groups are not done for the sake of coming into contact with teachers or leaders. Of course, Judaism directs us all to seek out a mentor, as we have already noted, but the group is something that's important in its own right. We are not told that only certain groups will facilitate our spiritual growth. We are told that every Torah class and every *minyan*, regardless of the individuals who form the whole, has the latent power to bring us to a level of closeness with God that we cannot attain on our own.

Group of Drunks

There's a saying in AA that the word "God" can also be read as an acronym that stands for "Group Of Drunks." In my experience, I have seen this concept misunderstood by those who would take it to what I consider useless extremes. On the one hand, there are those who decry the Group Of Drunks idea because, to them, it smacks of secular humanism, that it demeans the whole notion of belief in God. On the other hand, there are those who really do use the Group Of Drunks motto to argue that they need not grow in their faith and develop a relationship with God. Coming from a Jewish perspective as I do, it is hard for me to see what all the fuss is about. As the Chasidic saying goes, " 'You shall love your fellow as yourself' (Leviticus 19:18) is the vessel into which one draws down 'You shall love the Lord your God' (Deuteronomy 6:5)." This brings us to another topic.

To Whom Does God Speak?

I once heard an addict say, "God speaks to us all a little differently, hoping we'll tell each other." I have heard countless people in recovery express the sentiment, "God speaks through people." I cannot say what every one of them means by this, but the basic idea is certainly familiar to Judaism. The Talmud says, "The Omnipresent has many messengers to do his bidding," and Maimonides advises, as we already once mentioned in an earlier chapter, "Receive the truth regardless of its source." The Chasidic masters teach that everything that one sees and one hears is a teaching from God. Of course, some people teach us what to do and some teach us what not to do. But the fact remains, God uses us to serve as one another's guides, whether we know it or not.

When I first started speaking with people in recovery and listening to them share, I was struck by the poignancy of the spiritual message. But then I began to ponder how it is that the very same thought that I had come across in my religious studies but now heard spoken—albeit in different words—by another human being could have such a profound and transformative effect. If God's own word hadn't gotten the message across, how then could the words of a mere mortal, who merely spoke from his or her own experience? The answer is, of course, that even the most powerful spiritual ideas are worth little to us in dealing with everyday life if we have not internalized them. Often, it is only by hearing such truth spoken in simple, human terms, filtered through the mortal, finite mind of another human being, that brings the message home.

Strength in Numbers

A final word about the healing qualities of the group. I am reminded of King Solomon's eloquent words:

> Two are better than one, because they have good reward for their toil. For if they fall, one will lift up his friend; but woe to the one who falls and has no second one to lift him up. Moreover, if two lie down, they will have warmth, but how will one have warmth? And if a man prevails against the one, the two will stand against him. [Still greater than two is] a three-fold cord not easily broken. (Ecclesiastes 4:9-12)

Quite simply, we can do together what we cannot do alone. The Midrash says that the Jewish people are likened to reeds. A single reed is easily snapped in half, but a bundle of reeds cannot be broken. The philosophers call this *synergy*, a state wherein the whole is greater than the sum of its parts. Certainly, the group in cooperative recovery is a strong example of the exponential yield of synergetic bonding.

In mystical terms, a similar idea was expressed by Rabbi Dov Ber of Lubavitch, who said that when two Jews come together, there are two Godly souls against one animal soul. One of the basic doctrines of kabbalah is the idea of the duality of man's nature, that there are two souls, a Godly soul and an animal soul. Now, if two Jews come together, why should there be two Godly souls against one animal soul? Each one has both a Godly soul and an animal soul, so seemingly there should be two Godly souls against two animal souls. Even odds. The explanation given is that the animal soul is inherently selfish—it will not join with anyone or anything, even another animal soul, whereas the Godly soul is by nature selfless and loving and hence automatically gravitates toward uniting with others.

Perhaps we might say that a similar phenomenon occurs in the rooms of recovery. Each person's disease is focused on itself, while each person's spiritual side bonds with that which is redeeming in all of its fellows. Of course, this phenomenon does not always take place spontaneously. There are instances of groups being undermined by the unhealthy tendencies of one or a few individuals. Yet, remarkably, the Twelve-Step group somehow, seemingly organically, minimizes such ill effects and maximizes only the most positive contribution of each member. Somehow, most groups seem to gravitate toward a healthy state of interconnectedness and an adherence to the largely unspoken rule "Please, share your message and not your mess." All of this happens without experts guiding the process. It happens, I believe, because God has placed us together for a reason, and when individuals seek God together in humility and in earnest, the resulting product is something that clearly exceeds human potential. *It is a gift from Above to those who seek Him from below.*

Tolerance and Spiritual Health

Let's now look at the final teaching of the passage from the Mishnah. It begins, "Make for yourself a teacher," then says, "Acquire for yourself a friend," and concludes, "Judge every person favorably." (You may again wish to refer to the table on p. 92.)

As we have noted earlier, these three teachings cover the gamut of human relationships. In dealing with those whom we look up to, we apply the first teaching. When we encounter someone whom we relate to as a peer, we apply the second teaching. Finally, in what might be the most challenging task of all, when confronted with those in whom we see some glaring defect, we must carry out the third teaching and endeavor to judge them favorably.

Tolerance and goodwill to others is vital to recovery. The Big Book plainly states: "Resentment is the 'number one' offender. It destroys more alcoholics than anything else" (p. 64). Many old-timers will attest that a relapse is often preceded by feelings of indignation and intolerance. Thus, in recovery, just as one must have a teacher and a group of friends, it is crucial that one be accepting of all people. That does not mean that we have to make ourselves into the proverbial doormat. But what it does mean is that when we obsess on the wrongs that others have done us and see ourselves in the victim role, we remove ourselves from our relationship with God, for resentment and spiritual consciousness, as we shall explain, are diametric opposites of each other.

Faith and Resentment

The Talmud says that when one becomes angry, it is as if he serves idols. This is not mere hyperbole meant to make a point. Quite literally, anger is a rejection of God and lack of faith. If one believes that everything in this world comes from God and that God is in complete control, then one cannot *ever* be angry. Anger is a feeling of indignation toward a perceived injustice. We are angry when we feel that something shouldn't have happened the way that it did. But feeling outrage about something that has already happened to us is to argue with reality, which is to argue with God. Surely, the person of faith may at times express displeasure, disappointment, or even grief, for these are merely opinions. But there is a world of difference between saying, "I don't like the way things are," and saying, "Things really *shouldn't* be the way they are."

Now, how does this relate to interpersonal relationships? Rabbi Schneur Zalman explained that just as one must calmly accept the reality of a damage caused by an overt act of God, so must one have this same attitude when suffering at the hands of another person. Notwithstanding the fact that the offender may still be liable to God for his or her misdeed, what should concern us is that God already decreed the damage that came of the offender's poor choice. Surely it was not the offender's decision that caused the event to transpire, but rather, as with everything else in this world, it was brought about by God, even if for reasons known only to Him.

Accordingly, getting over our resentments is far more than a matter of unburdening ourselves of emotional pain. It is how we get in touch with God's purpose and plan for our lives. As long as we attribute to the actions of others any power to define our lives, then we submit ourselves to the tyranny of people, places, and things rather than placing ourselves in the care of God. Thus, even when there have been people in our lives who have intended us harm, our faith tells us that none of that could have ever derailed our lives from God's plan for us. To carry a resentment is to imagine that a created being has the kind of power over our lives that only God has. To forgive our enemies is to take away that power and to attribute it only to God.

Joseph and His Brothers

A perfect illustration of this kind of faith was displayed by Joseph toward his brothers. At the end of the Book of Genesis, we read that after the passing of Joseph's father, Jacob, Joseph's brothers, who had kidnapped him and sold him into slavery many years earlier, now fear that with their father gone, Joseph will take his vengeance on them. The brothers approach Joseph and beg him to do them no harm. Joseph is taken aback.

"Am I instead of God?" he asks rhetorically, "You intended evil for me but God meant it for good" (Genesis 50:19-20).

The words with which Joseph reassures his brothers are quite telling. Certainly, he could have said something to the effect of "two wrongs don't make a right." But Joseph communicated a message far more profound than that. Not only did he have no desire for revenge, he also would not concede to his brothers that they had even done anything to him for which he should feel wronged. He grants them that they had *intended* evil for him—for which they are presumably accountable before God—but that is none of his concern, as he says, "Am I instead of God?" As for what they actually *did* to him, Joseph completely dismisses any grounds for ill will.

In other words, Joseph explains the reason for his lack of resentment— that God was in control all along, and his brothers had done nothing to him that was outside of God's plan. To be sure, the day his brothers sold him as a slave, Joseph's life was changed forever. But God had a plan for him to come to Egypt, to become Pharaoh's viceroy, and to save his brothers in time of famine. That was certainly not what his brothers had in mind when they made their choice, but for Joseph, that was irrelevant. Life, as he saw it, was not a result of anything that any human being could do to him, but rather the culmination of God's omniscient and beneficent plan.

Dumping Resentments: A How-To

In the Fourth Step, the person in recovery is advised to take stock of his or her life and identify every source of pain and irritation. This detailed process known as a "Fourth Step inventory" entails looking back through one's life and noting any person against whom one still harbors any kind of ill feeling or grudge. The purpose is not to dredge up old pain but, to the contrary, to rid oneself of it.

The suggested format for the inventory is more or less as follows (see p. 111 for an example):

First, take a piece of paper and draw five columns.

Now, look back through your life, and write down any person, idea, or institution toward which you feel resentment or fear. This is Column 1. Do not go on to Column 2 until you have finished column 1. Hold nothing back.

Next, write down in every instance the reason or reasons that this person, idea, or institution causes you pain. This is Column 2.

After that, go down the list and note what aspect of your ego was threatened by the harm done. Was it your self-esteem, your security, your ambitions, your social standing?

Now, go down the list and, setting aside the fault of the other person, consider what possible role you might have had in making yourself available to be mistreated. Even if the other person is largely at fault, find your role. How did you put yourself out there to be hurt? The purpose is not to excuse the other person or to pretend that he or she is blameless. It's that analyzing the other person's fault is not germane here. This is *your* inventory to help *you* get better. The other person may very well need to do an inventory of his or her own, but that's none of your concern. At any rate, this is Column 4.

Finally, determine in each and every case which of your own character defects put you in a position to be hurt. Were you selfish, inconsiderate, self-seeking, fearful, or dishonest? This is Column 5.

Getting to the Root of Resentments

What I consider ingenious about the Fourth Step is that it uses our awareness of our negative feelings to get us to the root of our troubles—ourselves. We start out talking about others—which is always easy—but we end up making invaluable discoveries about our own nature—which are much harder to come by. From this position of self-discovery, we are empowered to make the only kind of real change that is ever possible—a change in ourselves.

In other words, the first column, where we list those toward whom we feel negatively, is not the main point. It is only a starting point. What will prove both enlightening and liberating is an examination of our own nature and how that has gotten us into trouble.

There is an old Chasidic story that expresses this idea marvelously. A Jew once visited the third Chabad Rebbe, Rabbi Menachem Mendel of Lubavitch, known as the Tzemach Tzedek, and complained that he was being disrespected by his fellow congregants in the synagogue. "They literally step all over me," he cried, to which the Rebbe gently responded, "If one spreads oneself out over the entire synagogue, then wherever others step, they are stepping on him."

As a rule, we get hurt where we have spread ourselves out. The hallmark of the truly selfless and humble person is not that he forgives easily but that he is impossible to offend in the first place. If we have been personally offended or hurt, that doesn't mean that we were necessarily "asking for it," but it does mean that if we want to avoid feeling slighted in the future, we will have to reduce our ego to a more useful size. An ego that is too big is always apt to be bumped and jostled by others. By coming to see exactly how and in what instances the ego has overextended itself, one can then address the very root and cause of the problem rather than trying to attack the symptoms.

Let's write an imaginary inventory for the fellow in the story. Given that we do not know the exact details, we will have to use a little bit of imagination.

Who or What	Why	Affects My	My Part	Defect of Character
The guys at my synagogue	They belittle me; show disrespect	Self-esteem, Security	I try to get too involved in everything that goes on	Self-seeking, Fear

After writing such an inventory, this fellow would be able to identify his real problem, his defect of character that got him into precisely the kind of situations where he would be likely to be mistreated. He would see that he had been self-seeking; that is, he was looking for recognition and validation. He would also see that he had felt fear. Perhaps he was afraid that if he did not voice his opinion on all matters, then his needs would be ignored. In trying to steal comfort for his fragile ego, he entered into an unhealthy situation with his peers.

If the fellow's experience writing an inventory was typical, he would find that even if he listed a hundred people in the first column of his Fourth Step list, he would come up with the same basic character defects in the last column over and over. At such a point, he would be in a much better position to set aside his feelings about what other people had done to him and start focusing on his own growth.

Compassion Cures

But what if even after having identified what one has to work on in oneself, one still can't let go of feelings of resentment toward others? Just because one is now focused on oneself doesn't mean that these bitter feelings will immediately disappear.

How are we to look upon those people who have wronged us or caused us pain? The Big Book suggests that one assume a totally new perspective of those who have hurt us—a perspective of compassion:

> Though we did not like their symptoms and the way these disturbed us, they, like ourselves, were sick too. We asked God to help us show them the same tolerance, pity, and patience that we would cheerfully grant a sick friend. When a person offended we said to ourselves, "This is a sick man. How can I be helpful to him? God save me from being angry. Thy will be done." We avoid retaliation or argument. We wouldn't treat sick people that way. If we do, we destroy our chance of being helpful. (p. 67)

Every one of us is to some extent spiritually and emotionally deficient. We all have character flaws. The greatest proof of this there can be is that we have caused someone pain. If we were 100 percent completely healthy, we would only spread kindness and good feelings to other people. In this light, we can view others who have hurt us as manifesting their own sickness. Again, knowledge of this fact does not excuse their behavior. But it does allow us to let go of the tiring work of condemning and censuring our fellow. When we carry around feelings of moral superiority, victimhood, and righteous anger, it is only we who lose. As they say, carrying resentment is like taking poison and waiting for the other person to die. To again quote the text of *Alcoholics Anonymous*:

> If we have been thorough about our personal inventory, we have written down a lot. We have listed and analyzed our resentments. We have begun to comprehend their futility and their fatality. We have commenced to see their terrible destructiveness. We have begun to learn tolerance, patience and good will toward all men, even our enemies, for we look on them as sick people. (p. 70)

Pray for Them

The Talmud relates a story about the great sage Rabbi Meir. A gang of thugs plagued his neighborhood and vexed him to no end. Apparently, their conduct became so egregious that Rabbi Meir thought it best to pray that the gangsters die. Before doing so, however, his wife, Berurya, spoke to him, quoting to her husband the verse in Psalms (104:35), "Let sins be uprooted from the earth, and the wicked will be no more."

She then proceeded to explain the verse as follows. It doesn't say that sinners should be uprooted but that the sins should be uprooted. "Do not pray that they die but that they should repent. Then, automatically, 'the wicked will be no more,' that is, they will no longer be wicked."

Rabbi Abraham Isaac Kook, the first Ashkenazic Chief Rabbi of Palestine under the British Mandate, explained that what Berurya was saying is that all people desire to be good. The fact that they are unable to do so reflects a sickness of the soul. Praying for such people is thus no different from praying for those who are physically ill and who despite their great desire to be healthy, cannot heal themselves without God's help.

As far as recovery is concerned, whether or not our prayers for our enemies will actually be effective in transforming them is somewhat immaterial. What is of vital importance is that compassion toward those who have harmed us shifts the paradigm. Feeling like a victim means toying with a false sense of entitlement that leads only to frustration and heartache. A person in recovery can scarcely afford to let someone else's problems compromise his or her own serenity. Taking a compassionate view of those who have harmed us allows us to take back the power that we have unwittingly granted such people in determining our own sense of well-being. It frees us from wasting our peace of mind on things we cannot control. As they say, "When you hold on to a resentment, you are giving somebody you don't even like rent-free space in your head."

Regular Maintenance

The Fourth Step is a major inventory, a comprehensive look at one's entire life that yields an acute understanding of one's most basic flaws and defects of character. Twelve-Step programs also advise that one continue to take inventory on a regular basis. The Tenth Step describes the need for a spot-check inventory that can be made at any time. Many people in recovery do so everyday, particularly at the end of the day before retiring at night.

The Tenth Step reads: "[We] continued to take personal inventory and when we were wrong promptly admitted it." Just as the Fourth Step inventory later serves as a basis for putting together an Eighth Step amends list, so, too, the regular Tenth Step inventory is meant to be followed up with amends whenever, wherever appropriate. The purpose of the Tenth Step is obvious—to make sure that new resentments don't begin to pile up.

As in the Fourth Step, where the focus is on oneself, the Tenth step also calls for humility. One ignores the other party's fault while endeavoring, in popular recovery parlance, to "keep our own side of the street clean." The objective is not to try to fix the other guy, but to rid oneself of feelings such as anger, fear, self-pity, and the like, all of which are antithetical to a strong and conscious faith in God. When unburdening oneself of this load, one cannot try to manage the other person's conduct, nor does one need to. As one fellow in recovery once told me, whenever he does a Tenth Step and sees that he needs to make peace with someone who may very well have been wrong, he asks himself to make a choice: "Do I want to be right, or do I want to be happy?"

The Bedtime Prayer

In Jewish practice, there is a prayer that one says upon retiring each night. Chasidic teachings particularly stress the importance that a *cheshbon ha-nefesh*—literally, "soul accounting"—be made on a regular basis, ideally at the end of each day. Thus, the bedtime prayer is seen as a time for daily, personal stocktaking.

In many customs, the prescribed bedtime ritual begins with following prayer:

> Master of the Universe! I hereby forgive anyone who has angered or vexed me, or sinned against me, either physically or financially, against my honor or anything else that is mine, whether accidentally or intentionally, inadvertently or deliberately, by speech or by deed, in this incarnation or in any other ...

Interestingly enough, it begins with a paragraph about forgiving those who have harmed us. Since the bedtime prayer is meant to serve as one's own personal stocktaking, why does it begin with calling to mind the offenses that one has suffered at the hands of others, even if it is for forgiving them? To one who is familiar with recovery, this should be an easy question to answer. We start our inventory by cataloging all of the ways in which other people have troubled us. But this is merely a jumping-off point. The result and true objective of this exercise is to place the onus for change squarely upon ourselves. Indeed, the prayer continues:

> May it will be Your will, Lord my God and the God of my forefathers, that I may sin no more and not repeat my sins . . . Whatever sins I have done before You, may You blot them out in Your abundant mercies . . .

How did we get from forgiving others for the harm they have done us to asking God to prevent *us* from sinning again? The other fellow is the sinner, right? He is the one who did us wrong. So why are we suddenly talking about *our* sins?

Just as in the story of the man who complained that everyone in his synagogue was stepping on him only to realize that he had spread himself out over the entire synagogue, so do we begin by recalling how we have been hurt by others only to end up asking God to erase our own transgressions. Pain and distress can be marvelous indicators of the areas of our lives that we are trying too hard to control. So, first we forgive others and let go of resentment. Then we turn all of those resentments around and gain insight into ourselves. This is a true "soul accounting."

The Miracles of Forgiveness

The Zohar relates a story that is the basis for the practice of reciting the "Master of the World" prayer before retiring at night.

Rabbi Abba, the scribe who wrote down the teachings of Rabbi Shimon bar Yochai that make up the Zohar, once sat at the gateway of the Town of Lud watching a traveler who was sitting upon a pile of rocks at the edge of a cliff. Exhausted from his journey, the man soon fell asleep. Rabbi Abba watched as a venomous snake made its way toward the sleeping man when, all of a sudden, a small animal jumped out and killed the snake. When the man stood up from his sleep, he saw the dead snake lying before him and got up to continue on his way. At that point, the pile of rocks upon which he had just been sitting tumbled over and fell straight over the edge of the cliff.

Rabbi Abba went up to the man and asked him, "Please tell me, what is it that you do that causes God to have just performed two miracles on your behalf, for it is not for naught that He has done so." Said the man to Rabbi Abba, "All my life I have never let a person harm me without trying to make peace with him and forgiving him. If I was unable to appease him, then I would not lie down in bed until I forgave him and anyone else who hurt me regardless of whatever harm they had done me. Finally, from then on, I would endeavor to do acts of kindness to that very person." Rabbi Abba began to cry and said, "This man's actions are greater than Joseph's, for Joseph forgave his brothers. Certainly a man forgives his own brothers. But this man forgives everyone who has harmed him. It is no surprise that God performs one miracle after another on his behalf."

The Miracle of Self-Transformation

By forgiving others, we may or may not see open miracles, as did the man Rabbi Abba saw. But what is certain is that by making peace with all people, even our enemies, we transcend our very nature. That in itself is a wonder of sorts.

What is a miracle, after all? A miracle is something that transcends the laws of nature. Indeed, that which is miraculous is deemed "supernatural"—above nature. Rising above our own nature is a miracle. The kind of psychic change and absolute transformation of personality that is possible through the Steps is nothing short of supernatural. That which medicine and therapy, arguing and reason, toughness and love, punishments, advice, and consequences could not accomplish has somehow inexplicably taken place. Is it any wonder, then, that we give all of the credit to God? Who else could have done this but He?

Recovery Meets the World

As a final word on the subject, it cannot be stressed enough how crucial to spiritual fitness is the ability to maintain healthy relationships with other people.

As most old-timers will tell you, "You didn't recover just so you could go to meetings." The true litmus test of spiritual strength is one's ability to face life. Recovery is a manner of living that must extend far beyond the one hour that one sits in a room full of people who all have spiritual growth in mind. As the Twelfth and culminating Step plainly states, "Having had a spiritual awakening as a result of these steps, we tried . . . to practice these principles in *all of our affairs.*"

I have heard many an old-timer advise that when having trouble with family members, coworkers, or friends, one should treat them as one would a newcomer to recovery—that is, with compassion, tolerance, patience, and understanding. It is in the group that those who come to recovery have their first experience of what it is like to connect peaceably and honestly with others. But the real application of this gift is when it is put to use in daily living. True spiritual consciousness is always consonant with and indistinguishable from being able to relate well to our fellow human beings.

A Yiddish expression humorously describes the person who tries to pursue spirituality while in isolation from others. *A tzaddik in peltz*—a saint in furs. As the Chasidic masters explain, when it is cold, you can either put on a fur coat or build a fire. In either case, you feel warm, but only by building a fire is there benefit for others.

It has been observed that the Ten Commandments were given on two equal-sized tablets. On the first tablet are written our obligations to God—"I am the Lord your God . . . You shall have no other gods . . ." and so on, while on the second tablet are written our obligations to humanity—Do not murder, steal, commit adultery, lie, or covet. The two tablets are equal. Indeed, they are the same. As the great sage Hillel once responded to a prospective convert who asked him to sum up the Torah in the amount of time that he could stand on one foot, "What is hateful to you, do not do to your fellow. This is the entire Torah; the rest is its commentary. Go and learn."

PART V
RECOVERY AND THE CODEPENDENT

How friends and family of addicts are affected by addiction ...
and how they, too, can recover.

CHAPTER 14
NAMING THE DISEASE

When Someone Else Is Your Whole Problem

I just got off the phone now.

I have had hundreds of almost identical conversations, but I want to write down what happened while it is still fresh in my mind, because it illustrates something I may not have the words to explain.

This section of the book, dealing with friends and family of addicts, is—for me—the most challenging subject to tackle. It is challenging because as much confusion and denial as there seems to be surrounding the issue of addiction, there must be ten times as much confusion and denial when it comes to recognizing and dealing with codependency.

So, let me tell you what just happened.

A woman called me to tell me that her husband is an alcoholic.

After giving her a few minutes to vent, I asked her whether she knew about the program of Al-Anon.

"It's a group for friends and family of alcoholics," I explained.

"And they can help me get my husband to stop drinking?"

"No," I said. "AA is for alcoholics. Al-Anon is for people who are going crazy from dealing with an alcoholic."

We went back and forth for a bit as she tried to understand what kind of help she needed other than to get her husband to stop drinking. Finally, I put it bluntly.

"Whether your husband wants to ruin *his* life or not is not your decision. How you live *your* life is your decision."

There was a long pause.

"You mean I should leave him?" she asked in a loud, dramatic whisper.

"I didn't say that. I said that how you live your life is your decision. Al-Anon can help you get some clarity about how to live your life."

"You mean whether or not I should stay with him."

"No. It's not really about him. With him or without him, you will always be with yourself. Right? Al-Anon can help you focus on your issues and work on yourself."

"You mean, if I change, my husband will stop drinking?"

"No, I mean if you change, then you will be better able to take care of yourself, whether or not he is still drinking. Al-Anon will help you to work on yourself."

"He's the sick one! Why do *I* have to work on myself?"

"You want to feel better; find a better way to live."

"I want him to stop drinking! Then I will be able to live!"

I have been through this exact conversation, almost word for word, countless times. I still find it heartbreaking.

This woman didn't need to tell me how crazy her life had become. She didn't have to tell me how she had been living for years with a constant and endless loop in her head saying, "When he stops drinking, life will be good. I must get him to stop, and life will be good. No matter what, I will get him to stop. When he stops drinking, life will be good." Neither did she need to tell me about the other endless loop saying, "This is the last time. You'll never let him do this again. You are going to leave him. This is the last time." These are the codependent's mantras—a mind-numbing sort of self-hypnosis, an automatic survival mode, constant loops playing in the mind. A life deferred to obsessive thoughts about someone else.

This is the insanity of addiction as it plays itself out in the life of the nonaddict. There is a name for this unmanageability. It's called *codependence*. There is recovery from codependence. But we have to recognize it first. We have to say its name.

The Codependent Profile

The Twelve-Step group Co-Dependents Anonymous (CoDA) has composed a list of typical patterns and characteristics of codependents that can be used as a tool for self-evaluation. The list, as it appears on the CoDA Web site, is as follows:

Patterns and Characteristics of Co-dependence

Denial Patterns:
I have difficulty identifying what I am feeling.
I minimize, alter, or deny how I truly feel.
I perceive myself as completely unselfish and dedicated to the well- being of others.
Low Self-Esteem Patterns:
I have difficulty making decisions.
I judge everything I think, say, or do harshly, as never "good enough."
I am embarrassed to receive recognition and praise or gifts.
I do not ask others to meet my needs or desires.
I value others' approval of my thinking, feelings, and behavior over my own.
I do not perceive myself as a lovable or worthwhile person.
Compliance Patterns:
I compromise my own values and integrity to avoid rejection or others' anger.
I am very sensitive to how others are feeling and feel the same.
I am extremely loyal, remaining in harmful situations too long.
I value others' opinions and feelings more than my own and am afraid to express differing opinions and feelings of my own.
I put aside my own interests and hobbies in order to do what others want.
I accept sex when I want love.
Control Patterns:
I believe most other people are incapable of taking care of themselves.
I attempt to convince others of what they "should" think and how they "truly" feel.
I become resentful when others will not let me help them.
I freely offer others advice and directions without being asked.
I lavish gifts and favors on those I care about.
I use sex to gain approval and acceptance.
I have to be "needed" in order to have a relationship with others.

Addicted to the Addict

There's an old joke. *Anyone* can be an addict, but to be a *codependent*, you've gotta *know* somebody!

Most of us have probably heard at some time that addiction is a "family disease." The addict is the most obvious symptom bearer—what psychologists call the "identified patient"—but anyone caught in the addict's chaotic existence is just as sick. This is not meant to spread blame. It's just a fact. And just as the addict is not at fault for being an addict, so, too, people who find themselves enmeshed in the addict's drama are not bad or weak either. Like the addict, they suffer from a malady of the mind, heart, and spirit. And just as the addict can recover, they, too, can recover.

Thus, contrary to popular misconception, those who join "Anon" groups, such as Al-Anon, Nar-Anon, and the like, are not there to learn how to cope better with the addict's problems. They are actually there to learn how to *stop* dealing with the addict's problems and start living their own lives—whether the addict chooses to recover or not. In other words, the addict is not the codependent's problem; the *codependent* is the codependent's problem. This explains what both statistics and experience have shown—that those who have been brought up in homes with addiction or who have been married to addicts and do not seek their own recovery almost invariably find themselves returning to relationships with still other addicts despite their most prodigious efforts to avoid it.

When we say that the codependent suffers from the disease of addiction just as much as the addict, we are not stating the obvious—that friends and family suffer from the consequences of the addict's behavior. We are talking about something that often goes unrecognized and hence untreated—*that friends and family of the addict are addicts themselves.* They may not be addicted to alcohol, drugs, gambling, sex, and so forth—although codependents can be addicts as well.

The codependent is *addicted to the addict.*

Controlling the Uncontrollable

As we mentioned a few times already in this book, one way of describing addiction is as an obsession with control. Regardless of one's drug of choice, all addictions stem from a deeply felt need to exercise an almost God-like power over reality. As such, active addicts expend inordinate amounts of energy trying to gain control over their addictions. In this regard, the codependent is no different—except that the codependent is fixated on controlling someone else's addiction, and the more hopeless the situation, the greater the codependent's compulsion to try to impose order.

Those unacquainted with the dynamics of codependency may find this baffling. If the codependent wants control, then why look for it amid chaos? But anyone who seriously poses this question might as well ask why the gambling addict is more likely to bet the house on the long shot than on the favorite. It is the heartbreaking futility of it all, the almost hopeless chance of beating the odds that seem to be so inexplicably enticing.

In other words, codependency, like addiction, is the obsession with controlling the uncontrollable—or, quite literally, to die trying. There is also a certain morbid sense of nobility in the codependent's dedication to living out every horrid detail of their script to its tragic end. The codependent will expend extraordinary efforts to avoid "letting go"—something that he or she sees as an unforgivable betrayal.

Indeed, much like the addict, the codependent is often a romantic and an idealist. Both addicts and codependents are prone to act recklessly in pursuing their wistful dreams of perfection, and both seem to have an uncanny knack for quickly forgetting or justifying the dire consequences of their indiscretion. In this way, addicts and codependents are often drawn into living out *each other's* unrealistic fantasies. Thus goes the old joke: "How do you know when an addict and a codependent are on a second date? There's a U-Haul in the driveway."

Lack of Identity

One of the defining components of the codependent personality is the lack of self-concept. Hence, another old joke told in recovery circles— "What's the last thing to happen to a codependent before they die? Someone else's life flashes before their eyes."

The field of psychology may offer insight into *why* a person fails to develop an adequate sense of identity, but in recovery we are more interested in *how* it affects the individual in the present. Whatever the cause for the codependent's lack of identity, what is certain is that the unrecovered codependent faces a vicious cycle of seeking validation and receiving abuse and degradation instead. I once heard a recovering codependent sum up the story of his life as being "just like that old country western song—'looking for love in all the wrong places.'"

As we alluded to at the beginning of this chapter, codependency is quite similar to and in some ways even indistinguishable from addiction.

One thing that addiction and codependence have in common is that they are both forms of being divorced from one's own self. The addict uses his or her drug of choice as an escape. The codependent uses the preoccupation with trying to "fix" the addict in much the same way.

The Chasidic master, Rabbi Zushya of Anipoli is said to have bemoaned on his deathbed, "When I come before the heavenly tribunal, I am not afraid they will demand of me, 'Zushya, why weren't you Moses?' I am afraid lest they ask me, 'Zushya, why weren't you Zushya?' "

Each of us has been give a unique mission in this world and a lifetime to carry it out. The active codependent, however, puts life on hold while trying everything to change the addict. The codependent manipulates, argues, prays, screams, cries, makes ultimatums with the addict, makes ultimatums with God, but the one thing that the codependent does not do—*cannot* do without the help of a Higher Power—is let go. The codependent can no more imagine life without the addict than the addict can imagine life without addiction.

Of course, it is not the codependent's true mission in life to change the addict—it is the *addict's* mission in life to change the addict—thus, the codependent lives in a state of disconnect from his or her own God-given purpose. Obviously, such an existence is the very picture of futility and frustration.

Often, the codependent's greatest hurdle is to accept that he or she can and must recover even if the addict does not. There may be a happy life for the codependent living with an addict, but there is no happiness and no life for the codependent *addicted* to the addict.

In practical terms, this means that if the codependent can safely, serenely continue a relationship with the addict without neglecting his or her own needs, then that is the codependent's *choice*. But if the codependent ignores his or her own safety and well-being just to keep the addict around, then that is not a choice—that is a *compulsion*. The codependent may call it love or loyalty or a commitment to working things out. But what it is, in reality, is two frightened people giving each other an excuse not to live their lives as their true selves.

The Intimacy Cripple

The paradox of codependency is that while it expresses itself in the form of a relationship with another person, it is the complete opposite of a relationship. Codependency is actually the inability to relate genuinely to another human being. Indeed, both codependents and addicts are often described as "intimacy cripples."

I once heard a codependent laughingly describe his failed method for finding true love—"Find the most superficially desirable person who will have you, make up a personality for that person, then stick to it no matter what!" As long as we cannot accept ourselves and others for who we are, there is no true intimacy, as the saying goes, "Addicts don't have relationships; they take hostages!" To put it simply, a codependent relationship is one which *simulates* intimacy, with none of its rewards but all of its dramatic intensity.

Another one of the great Chasidic masters, the Rabbi of Kotzk, once said, "If I am me because I am me, and you are you because you are you, then I am me, and you are you. However, if I am me because you are you, and you are you because I am me, then I am not me, and you are not you!"

What this means is that if I have an autonomous identity, then I can be involved in a real relationship with another person. However, if I look to the relationship to gain my identity, then neither of us is connecting to the other.

In other words, the basis for the inability to relate to others is the inability to relate to self. The codependent, as we have already mentioned, has a profound lack of self-concept, which manifests as emotional dependence on others. This desperate search for personal identity makes it impossible to experience a genuinely intimate relationship.

Codependents, just like addicts, are actually "emotionally unavailable" to enter into a relationship. The only difference is that whereas the antisocial aspect of addiction may be more apparent, the fact that the codependent is equally unavailable for intimate relationships can be harder to detect. The addict's unsavory shenanigans clearly mark him or her as someone who—to borrow a phrase from kindergarten report cards—"does not play well with others," even as the codependent may seem like a devoted or caring spouse, parent, friend, sibling, and so forth. But this ability to fool others is of no benefit to the codependent. It only serves to provide the needed cover for the codependent to persist wasting his or her life away in an unhealthy situation while appearing all the while to be the normal one.

If I Am Not for Myself . . .

A two-thousand-year-old Torah teaching seems to describe both the problem and the solution for the codependent rather well.

The Mishnah records that the sage Hillel used to teach: "If I am not for myself, who will be? But if I am only for myself, what am I? And if not now, when?"

These are three short phrases, each one a question. Let us first examine the first part of Hillel's teaching. "If I am not for myself, who will be?" The simple meaning of this rhetorical question is an admission that I must be assertive in taking care of my own needs because I cannot expect other people to do it for me. This is one of the dilemmas of codependence. Friends and family of addicts often suffer from a fundamental lack of self-concept and, as such, have a very hard time recognizing their own needs. They focus on fixing, changing, rescuing, blaming the addict but rarely, if ever, look at what they can do for themselves. Recovery from codependency is thus a process of discovering an identity and a life outside of the dysfunctional relationship with the addict—becoming one's own nurturer and advocate.

To return to Hillel's statement, the classical commentaries explain that the question "If I am not for myself, who will be?" may also be interpreted in a slightly different manner—"If I don't *fix* myself, who will fix me?" In other words, if I am not accountable to myself for my own growth and development, who else's job is it?

In the case of the codependent, both interpretations of Hillel's statement are on the mark. In recovery, codependents learn not only to take care of their own needs, but also, more important, to work on their own self-refinement. Indeed, the former can be dependent on the latter. A popular phrase among recovering codependents is, "Keep the focus on yourself." It is by first developing a sense of personal responsibility that codependents ultimately learn to set healthy boundaries and to respect themselves. Only by focusing on what they need to change in themselves, instead of in others, do they eventually gain the requisite self-respect to be able to take care of themselves as well.

In so doing, the codependent is then able to fulfill the second part of Hillel's teaching—"But if I am only for myself, what am I?" This is the call to helping others. It is by *first* establishing a sense of emotional autonomy that the codependent becomes able to "be for others," namely, to give freely and lovingly. It is perhaps the great paradox of codependency that as much as unrecovered codependents are obsessed with helping other people, they are actually incapable of truly giving. *Active codependents do not share their love; they trade it.* They have a very hard time seeing love as anything else but a bargaining chip to be cashed in for safety, security, and validation. They are typically obsessed with making themselves irreplaceable in someone else's life. In recovery, the codependent discovers that he or she is an intrinsically worthy child of God who can love others altruistically without any need for reward.

Let's look now at the last of Hillel's three questions. The ultimate victory in recovery from codependence is when the codependent sees the fruition of Hillel's third teaching—"And if not now, when?" Rather than waiting for the addict to get better or for the fulfillment of any other condition that the codependent has placed on happiness, the codependent embraces life and lives fully in "the now." Nobody and nothing need be any different from what they are at this moment, for, as the codependent comes to learn, we are free at all times to choose peace of mind and happiness for ourselves regardless of the choices that other people make for themselves.

	Hillel's Phrase	Meaning
First Question	If I am not for myself, who will be?	I must tend to my own needs . . . (alternatively) I must tend to my own fixing . . .
Second Question	If I am only for myself, what am I?	then I will be able to give to others as an act of intimacy . . .
Third Question	If not now, when?	and see that I can choose happiness for myself now, regardless of conditions.

CHAPTER 15
GOD AND THE CODEPENDENT

Inhuman Perfection vs. Human Imperfection

Just as with the recovery from any addiction, recovery from codependence is based on forming a dynamic relationship with God.

You see, in a very real way, the codependent is committing emotional *idolatry*—that is, feeling that someone or something has God-like control over reality. The codependent alternately attributes superhuman power to his or her own self and to the addict. The spiritual basis for recovery from codependency is thus to let go of the maddening pursuit of inhuman perfection and to embrace human imperfection. God is perfect. The rest of us—addicts, codependents, and everyone else—are all just doing the very best we can with what we have.

God-consciousness is the foundation of a new life and a new perspective of reality, for as long as one is devoted to an imaginary vision of perfection, it is impossible to live contentedly in the real world. One must instead learn to trust in the only true perfection—an all-powerful God who is always perfectly in control.

We may not *like* reality. That's okay. We are entitled to our opinion. But the fact is that everything is always the way it needs to be, at least for right now.

We are not God. We cannot be. We don't need to be.

We cannot control what other people do. And what other people do should not control us.

Don't Walk in Front of Me

There is a popular Jewish children's song that I learned from my kids who learned it in camp:

Don't walk in front of me, I may not follow,
Don't walk behind me, I may not lead;

Just walk beside me and be my friend,
And together we will walk in the ways of Ha-Shem.

Ha-Shem is a Jewish expression for God. It literally means "The Name." Because we don't ever understand God but need to call Him something, we call him "The Name"—in other words, "Whoever He Is."

I think this is a real recovery song, especially regarding codependence.

"Don't walk in front of me, I may not follow." I cannot define my life by your decisions. I will not choose to put my happiness in your hands. I will not spy on you, monitor you, or try to control your behavior. Neither will I chase you nor cling to you. I am not waiting for you to look over your shoulder to make sure that I am still there. I have to walk my own path.

"Don't walk behind me, I may not lead." I cannot take responsibility for your happiness, security, or well-being. I am not going to set the tone of this relationship. I am just hewing my own path, and you are free to do as you please. Don't expect me to have things figured out, because I am often wrong. Do not rely on me to be able to make things right, because I do not have that kind of power.

"Just walk beside me and be my friend, / And together we will walk in the ways of Ha-Shem." If you want to be my equal and join me as I seek the God of my understanding, I am open and available for this. I am not in charge, and neither are you. We're both on a journey where God is both the way and the destination.

Emotional Cannibalism

To sum up what we've just said: a codependent relationship may be described as one where two people try to use each other to connect to themselves and fail, whereas a healthy relationship is one where two people connect to God through each other and succeed.

There is a teaching of the sages in the Mishnah that describes this dynamic perfectly:

Rabbi Chanina, deputy high priest, would say, "Pray for the welfare of the kingship, for were it not for the reverence [it commands,] people would swallow each other alive." Rabbi Chananya ben Teradyon would say, "... If two sit together and exchange words of Torah, the Divine Presence rests between them. . . ."

The Lubavitcher Rebbe explained how this teaching may be understood on a psychospiritual level as a description of the difficulty in maintaining healthy relationships. Rabbi Chanina, deputy high priest, does not say that if not for the fear of the kingship people would kill each other. To the contrary, he says that they would "swallow each other alive." Swallowing someone alive implies subsuming another person within one's own desires. The other person remains alive—he thinks and feels—but he is "swallowed" within another.

The only thing that prevents this from happening is "the reverence of the kingship," which the Rebbe interprets accordingly to mean the Godly Kingship. If we are talking about emotional cannibalism, there is no government that can prevent that. What keeps us from devouring one another is proper reverence for the Divine.

In recovery language, if I am relying on my own power to make life as I think it ought to be, then I must control you. If, on the other hand, I am relying on God's Power and putting myself in His care, then I have room for you to be as you are. There can be intimacy instead of smothering; vulnerability instead of overpowering. All this is possible, though, only when we are mindful of God.

This is the connection to the teaching that follows—"Rabbi Chananya ben Teradyon would say, 'If two sit together and exchange words of Torah, the Divine Presence rests between them.' " When we come together as equals, when there is open communication and a healthy give-and-take between us, then we know that God's Presence is among us.

The Fixer

Two addicts and a codependent are in line to be executed at the guillotine. It's just a joke, so don't ask why they're being executed. Anyway, the first addict puts his head down on the block, the rope is cut, and the blade comes whizzing downward only to jam in its track an inch above his neck. The executioner says that according to law, the addict is now free to go. Next, the second addict is up. He puts his head down on the block, the rope is cut, and again the blade is stuck an inch above his neck. He, too, is let go. Finally, it's the codependent's turn at the guillotine. As he steps up to the platform, he taps the executioner on the shoulder, points, and says, "You know, I think I can fix that."

There is an amazing story in the Book of Genesis about the reunion between Joseph and his brothers. We spoke about this story a little bit in a previous chapter when discussing resentments. Well, let's look at another part of the story now, the part when Joseph sees his beloved baby brother, Benjamin, for the first time in many years. "And he [Joseph] fell on his brother Benjamin's neck, and cried; and Benjamin cried on his neck" (Genesis 45:14).

Aside from the obvious interpretation, tradition sees a deeper significance to their weeping. Joseph mourned prophetically over the Holy Temple in Jerusalem, which would one day be built in the land apportioned to the tribe of Benjamin. Benjamin cried over the Sanctuary at Shiloh, which he foresaw would stand in the territory apportioned to the tribe of Joseph. Since both holy houses were destined to be destroyed, each brother wept for the other's loss.

This interpretation raises a question: Why did each one cry over the *other's* future calamity? They faced similar fates. Why then did they not both cry for *themselves*?

The answer lies in the world of difference between how the Torah teaches us to regard our own disasters as opposed to those of our fellow human beings.

When we see someone else heading toward destruction, we can offer love, encouragement, and support so that they might have more strength to get out of their mess, but ultimately we cannot solve their problems for them. Each of us holds the key to finding our own solution. Thus, when we have truly done our part, and disaster is still looming, the only thing left to do is cry; not with tears of anger or frustration, mind you, but tears of genuine sympathy and compassion. We do not speak condemningly, and we do not judge; neither are we aloof nor unfeeling. We simply admit that the outcome is not up to us. We pray, we release with love, and we cry, because there is nothing else left to do.

When it comes to our personal destruction, however, we dare not tearfully resign ourselves to our own demise. There is no time for weeping. We must act, for we have no right to give up hope and to shirk responsibility for ourselves.

Recovery teaches us to be gracefully compassionate toward others while being firm with ourselves, for we can only fix ourselves, not others. The Midrash says that when a rooster has fallen in a pile of dirt, a thousand people with a thousand combs cannot clean him, but if the rooster gives himself one good shake, he casts off every speck of dust.

Detachment

The key is to detach, which, by the way, is another recovery acronym—"Don't Even Try And Change Him/Her."

As we have just explained, using the story of Joseph and Benjamin as an illustration, detachment does *not* mean a lack of compassion. To the contrary, for the codependent, detachment is actually the *only* way to feel pity—rather than toxic hatred—for the addict.

But this, again, requires reliance on a Higher Power.

Recovering codependents talk about "releasing the addict to the care of God." For someone whose whole identity is intertwined with dealing with someone else's problems, the only solution seems to be admitting that it is up to God to take care of the addict.

This, for the codependent, is also an admission of his or her own humanity. Al-Anon talks about the "Three Cs" of recovery—"I didn't Cause it; I can't Cure it; I can't Control it." Coming to terms with this means accepting one's own limitations, one's ultimate inability to play God.

There is a recovery catch phrase—"Let go, and let God." This is true about everything, but for the recovering codependent, it is especially important that he or she learn how to let go of the *addict*.

The Victim's Disease

If the codependent's problem is obsession with control, then the solution is to learn how to give up control—specifically to release the addict to the loving and all-capable care of a Higher Power, and to generally accept God's omnipotent control over all aspects of life.

However, one of the greatest obstacles to making this decision is that the codependent may actually feel that controlling others is a *moral obligation*. It's lonely and exhausting playing a constant game of "Aha! I've caught you!" but that's the price for retaining the moral high ground, right?

There's a famous expression that you hear a lot in recovery—Do you want to be right or do you want to be happy?

Part of recovering and trusting in God is to allow God to deal with the "sinners." I don't think it's any coincidence that the most God-conscious people I know are also the most tolerant. Volunteering to be a member of the morality police is usually a sign of spiritual sickness.

The Cat and the Homeowner

One of my teachers in rabbinical school once asked us, "Boys, we all know that both the cat and the homeowner hate the mouse. So, what's the difference between the cat and the homeowner? The homeowner hates the mouse and is happier when there is no mouse. The cat hates the mouse, but doesn't know what to do with himself when the mouse is gone."

An outside observer who is ignorant of a cat's nature might think that the cat would be a lot happier if we were to get rid of the mouse. So, too, many people think that codependents will magically get better if they are separated from the addict. But the codependent's recovery has nothing to do with the mouse. The codependent's recovery is about learning to be a cat that can stretch out in the sunshine and let the homeowner deal with the mice. And if God is the Homeowner, then He has a loving plan for mice, too. And that is no concern of the cat's.

The Zealot

There is a story in the Book of Numbers about the High Priest Aaron's grandson, Phinehas. A prominent Israelite leader was actively encouraging immorality among the people, so Phinehas took the law into his own hands. He killed him.

It was later determined that under the circumstances, Phinehas had acted within the law. Many people, nonetheless, started to examine his motives. Technically, his act was permitted, they admitted, but he was obviously just a vicious brute who had simply bided his time waiting for the opportunity to kill under protection of the law, wasn't he? Many of his countrymen started playing armchair psychologist, analyzing issues that he may have picked up from his family of origin. His maternal grandfather, they pointed out, was Jethro, a convert, who before having become a Jew was an idolatrous priest who fattened calves to be slaughtered as sacrifices to strange gods. Surely, Phinehas had inherited this cruelty and bloodlust from his mother's father.

The Torah is thus quick to point out that Phinehas had another grand-father, on his father's side, Aaron the High Priest (Numbers 25:11). We know that when Aaron passed away, the people mourned him more than they did the passing of his brother, Moses. Aaron was beloved by the people because he had a reputation as a diplomat, one who strove to make peace between man and his fellow. The Torah tells us that, far from being naturally violent or belligerent, Phinehas had actually inherited the peace-loving demeanor of his paternal grandfather, Aaron.

But why is this important? What if Phinehas did enjoy being a vigilante?

That is precisely the point. The lesson for the ages is that one who is naturally inclined to judge others harshly may *not* act as a zealot. That is why the Torah goes out of its way to specifically trace Phinehas' lineage to Aaron. It was Phinehas' nature to be tolerant and forgiving. He did not, as some do, seek out opportunities for righteous anger. That is why he was able to act as a zealot. As a teacher of mine once explained to me, "If you actually want to be a zealot, then you are not one."

Tough Love

There's another important lesson, I think, to be learned from this story. The leader whom Phinehas killed—his name was Zimri—was destroying the familial core of the Jewish nation. Zimri had encouraged his kinsmen to consort openly with Midianite harlots, who seduced them into wor-shipping idols. The nation had no idea how to deal with the confusion. Even Moses and Aaron were silent. In many ways, this episode reads like the story of a family thrown into chaos by the madness of addiction.

The Torah makes it clear that the one who put a stop to the mayhem was not acting out of anger or intolerance, not some unhinged and hysteri-cal fanatic, but a person who acted deliberately and mindfully.

In the entire Torah, this is the only story of vigilante justice. Judaism has never been a religion of militant extremism, and in the one and only case in which an act of zealotry does occur, the most unlikely person to do so carries it out. The lesson is that although there may be situations that demand "tough love," the toughness must come from love. Those who act out of anger or fear do not put an end to disorder but only add to it. Those who are prone to indignation and outrage are incapable of doing anything but countering madness with still more madness. To return to our analogy, when there is a mouse in the house, unleashing the cat only fills the home with more chaos. Only the compassionate and the tolerant—those who have relinquished their emotional stake in the drama—can act decisively and break the cycle.

There is a beautiful prayer from the Al-Anon book *As We Understood*, which I think says it all:

> I cannot control or change my friends or loved ones, so I release them into Your care for Your loving hands to do with as You will. Just keep me loving and free from judging them. If they need changing, God, You'll have to do it; I can't. Just make me willing and ready to be of service to You, to have my shortcomings removed, and to do my best. (p. 215)

CHAPTER 16
THE STUBBORN AND REBELLIOUS SON

Inheritance

Have you ever seen that bumper sticker? "Insanity is hereditary. You get it from your kids."

I think many parents of addicts would agree.

The funny thing is, I think the opposite is true. I think—and this is just my take on things—that addiction is hereditary in the sense that a child who is an addict gets it from a parent who is a codependent.

Please note that I'm using the term hereditary very loosely here. I'm not trying to take a stand on the nature vs. nurture/environment vs. genetics debate about what causes addiction. I really have no idea which one it is. It's probably a combination of both. What I *am* saying is that contrary to popular misconception, a parent doesn't "suddenly" become a codependent because the kid grows up and becomes an addict. It's the other way around. Parents who are codependents tend to raise addicts. It shouldn't be hard to understand. We know that codependents tend to date and marry addicts. So, it should make even more sense that codependents tend to raise addicts. I mean, whom do you have more influence on than your kids?

Before we get rolling, I'd also like to insert this disclaimer. I do not wish to give the impression that the development of the addictive personality comes about exclusively as the result of the codependent behavior of a parent. Addiction may be brought on by many factors – *including*, but certainly not limited to, the intersection of the child's personality with the personalities and parenting styles of the parents. Obviously, not *all* children of codependent parents become addicts and/or codependents themselves. What I am saying is that the connection between codependent parents and their addict children is one that is all too often misinterpreted or ignored.

Even with such a disclaimer, this is still a very difficult point to get across. It meets a lot of resistance, I think, because there is almost nobody who can elicit more pity and sympathy than the parent of an addict. To the outside observer, the mother or father of an addict is an absolute picture of martyrdom, a hapless victim of rotten luck.

But I want to tell you what most "insiders" know. For virtually every young addict who is on the road to self-destruction, there is a parent who inadvertantly put the kid on that path.

I know, it sounds crazy. Maybe even mean-spirited. But it's true. And like all truth, it can be found in the Torah if we look for it. I believe that the Torah describes the dynamics of the codependent parent and in so doing teaches us how to understand and—with God's help—find ways to heal this condition.

A Biblical Case Study
What follows is a literal translation of Deuteronomy 21:18-21:

> If a man will have a stubborn and rebellious son, who will not obey the voice of his father, or the voice of his mother, and though they chastened him, will not listen to them, then his father and his mother will seize him, and bring him out to the elders of his city, and to the gate of his place; and they will say to the elders of his city, "This son of ours is stubborn and rebellious, he will not obey our voice; he is a glutton and a drunkard." Then all the men of his city shall stone him to death. So shall you remove the evil from your midst, and all Israel shall hear and fear.

I know. It's not very politically correct. It's got stoning in it and everything. But if we can withhold the knee-jerk reactions to the perceived brutality of the story, we can learn much here. First, it's very interesting that the sages say that this scenario is actually put forth as a purely hypothetical case. According to one opinion, the Torah is not describing here something that would ever actually happen. Rather, it is outlining a theoretical scenario for presenting a didactic model. As the Talmud says, the story is taught not for practical purposes but "so that we may study it and reap reward."

In other words, the law calling for the execution of the stubborn and rebellious son was never intended to be carried out. Indeed, the Talmud makes clear that the detailed legal parameters that determine who is or is not a stubborn and rebellious son are actually so complex that it would be, for all practical purposes, impossible for all of the necessary criteria to ever be met. The story is meant to serve as an illustration of certain principles; an archetype where disastrous consequences are hypothetically played out to their terrible end so that future generations may gain insight and hopefully learn how to put a stop to such madness should it rear its head in their families.

Whose Story?

Let's take a closer look at the verses.

It may surprise you, but the story doesn't begin with a stubborn and rebellious son. It begins with a father to whom there will be a son—"*If a man will have* a stubborn and rebellious son . . ."

It's an easy detail to miss, but it makes all the difference in the world. The Torah tells us right away that the "problem child" is not really the main character in this drama. The father is. Sure, we all *think* of this as a story about a stubborn and rebellious son. But it's really the story of a father—a father trying to raise his son.

Usually, it will be some drama in the addict's life that gets a family to admit that things are out of hand. But once the family does find help, it is also almost instantly clear that the addict is not the only sick person or even the sickest person in the family.

It makes sense that the Torah doesn't really tell the story of a stubborn and rebellious son so much as the story of his parents. In fact, the son actually does nothing in the whole story. He says nothing and he takes no action. The only thing the Torah actually tells us about him is that he doesn't listen to his parents. The rest of the details we only hear secondhand when his parents complain to the elders.

The parents, not the son, are the principal actors in this narrative. It is they who enlist the aid of the elders; it is they who press the issue and bring the whole drama to its gruesome conclusion.

Let's follow the story along verse by verse and see how that happens.

Breakdown of the Codependent Marriage

The first verse in this narrative tells us that the stubborn and rebellious son "will not obey the voice of his father or the voice of his mother."

The word for "obey" or "heed" can actually be read as "listen," so that it says that the son literally "is not listening" to his parents. But the same word could also be translated as "hear," so that it says he does not "hear" his parents. In other words, it is possible that this is a home where there is no real parental authority. It is *not* that the child hears and then *rejects* his parents' orders, it's that there is no parental voice to be heard in the first place.

Another extremely fascinating detail about this family is hinted in the seemingly redundant wording "voice of his father" and "voice of his mother." Why not just say "his father and mother's voice"? Why? Because the parents are not unified, hence there is no singular "father and mother's voice." There is instead a "voice of his father" and a "voice of his mother."

It is extremely important to note in this regard that the problems in the marriage faced by the parents of an addict usually predate the manifestation of the addicted child's problem. The parents weren't on the same page long before the kid ever came along. Now that they are trying to co-parent together and failing, it becomes more *evident* that there is discord in their relationship, but the child didn't *cause* the breakdown of the marriage. To the contrary, raising a child who is an addict is the *result* of their lack of emotional support for one another as husband and wife.

Of course, later, when the parents take their son to the elders, the story that they tell is quite different—"He will not obey *our* voice." They are either lying or in denial—or a little bit of both—about what their home is really like. There is a little tinge of victimhood there, too. "We're good parents, but *he* won't listen!" But we're getting ahead of ourselves.

Ineffective Discipline

The second thing the Torah tells us about the parents' relationship with their son is that "though they chastened him, [he] will not listen to them." There is a saying of the sages, "Words from the heart enter the heart." It is for this reason that the Chasidic masters say that if one rebukes another and the rebuke is rejected, it is the fault of the rebuker. If one would only rebuke sincerely, then his or her words would be accepted.

In other words, the fact that the way they "chasten" their son has proved ineffective tells us much more about their style of discipline than it does about the son's behavior. The parents need to learn how to discipline their child.

This in itself would not be such a great problem—I mean, it could be dealt with—if the parents would just learn how to set and enforce limits for their child. But that's not what happens. What do the parents do? They "seize" their child and "bring him out to the elders." The drama is starting to build. The parents now have other people involved. They've brought in experts. It's becoming a community uproar.

Enmeshment

Before we go on and talk about what the parents tell the elders, I want to go back to that word "seize" again. Talk about a classic inability to let go. The parents literally *seize* their child. They aren't interested in parenting. They want control.

What makes this more absurd and more obviously dysfunctional is that one of the many conditions of actually being tried as a stubborn and rebellious son is that the "child" isn't really a child at all.

In Jewish law, there is no criminal action that can be taken against a minor. Torah determines that a boy becomes a "moral adult"—that is, he has the intellectual capacity to know between right and wrong—at thirteen. This is the status known as "bar-mitzvah," which literally means one who is obligated in the commandments. In our society we may scoff at the idea of a thirteen-year-old being considered an adult, but, I think, that is because in our very materialistic society, we think of adulthood as synonymous with being financially independent. Judaism, which sees adulthood as a moral issue, designates it as the point at which you are held responsible for your own actions. But I digress. *The stubborn and rebellious son is an adult.* Why are his parents taking him to the elders? If the parents really don't know what to do with him, let them kick him out of the house. Does that sound harsh? It's a lot less harsh than what is going to happen after they have their son sentenced and executed based on their testimony. The parents are *seizing* their child and refusing to let go. They are the ones who turn this whole situation *literally* into a capital case.

The Talmud explains that what is meant by the parents' charge that their son is "a drunkard and a glutton" is that he steals money from them in order to buy food and wine, which he then consumes in bad company. These are not capital crimes. If the parents really want to take legal action against their son, let them turn their son in as a thief to be punished accordingly. The rabbis could even force him to pay back the money. But the parents don't go to the authorities to turn in a thief who happens to be their son. They go to the elders and say, "This son of ours is stubborn and rebellious, and will not obey our voice." Instead of making a legal claim, they start complaining about their family problems. "This son of ours . . ."

Moreover, rather than just describing the *behavior*, they assail their son's *character*, his *being*. They label and blame. "This son of ours *is* stubborn and rebellious . . . *is* a glutton and a drunkard."

It should be noted that the court will not execute the son the first time his parents bring him in. The law is that they must bring him to the elders *three times*. Each time, they return home with their son. Each time they bring him back to the elders to complain some more. You would think that after the first couple of times, the parents would get the picture. The truth is, if they were rational, then they would. Normal, healthy parents would not have their son executed for being stubborn and rebellious. But these parents can't stop. Their involvement is compulsive. They are ensnared in the drama.

You know another thing? The law stipulates that the food and wine that the son consumes must be bought with money stolen from his parents and consumed while standing on their property. *So why is he still living in the house?!* If the parents can't handle him, they should have him leave. But this is classic enabling, that is, denial *and* enabling. Because the enablers will say, "We *are* being tough. We keep grabbing him and bringing him to the elders!" Not only can't they dissociate from the situation, *they* are the ones pushing the situation to its dramatic conclusion.

Scripture (Deut. 21:18–21)	Possible Interpretation
If a man will have a stubborn and rebellious son	Parent plays the main role in the drama
who will not obey the voice of his father, or the voice of his mother	Discord in the marriage predates problems with the child
and though they chastened him, will not listen to them	Ineffective disciplining
then his father and his mother will seize him	Enmeshment
and bring him out to the elders of his city, and to the gate of his place	Building drama
and they will say to the elders of his city	Laying blame
"This son of ours is stubborn and rebellious	Labeling
he will not obey our voice	Denial about what goes on in the home
he is a glutton and a drunkard."	Labeling
Then all the men of his city shall stone him to death.	Illustration of ultimate fate if parents continue this way
So shall you remove the evil from your midst, and all Israel shall hear and fear.	The lesson to us

The Predictable Outcome

The classic question that is asked about the stubborn and rebellious son is why he has to be killed. It does seem like an excessive reaction to his relatively petty transgressions. The easy answer—a false answer—is that it's just a hypothetical case. But that doesn't really answer the question. The fact that it's theoretical doesn't make it any less extreme.

The classic answer is thus that the stubborn and rebellious son is not executed because of his present but because of his inevitable future. Eventually, he will not be able to steal enough money from his parents to support his growing habit and will resort to a life of crime wherein he will inevitably kill somebody. It is deemed better that he die now while still innocent than later when he is guilty.

I want to offer my own interpretation of this explanation. Most people seem to understand that the stubborn and rebellious son is put to death as a preventive measure. But, as we said, the story is purely illustrative. What would it be preventing? And why hasten the inevitable, anyway?

The story of the stubborn and rebellious son makes a point. What is that point? And to whom is it being made?

In so many words—"Parents, you are killing your child."

I don't take those words lightly, and neither does anyone who has ever had to actually say those words to another person. Yet, anyone who deals with addiction knows how predictable these things are. Anyone who has seen it a few times already knows how it's going to end.

So, the Torah says to these hypothetical parents of this hypothetical son in this hypothetical story, "Mom and dad, it's the third time now you've come to us to complain about your adult son's behavior. Things haven't gotten better since you've come here; they've only gotten worse. Here's where this is heading. There is only one way that this is going to end, and now we will *show* you what that is."

When the account concludes "so shall you remove the evil from your midst, and all Israel shall hear and fear," I don't think it's just talking about the results of executing this hypothetical stubborn and rebellious son. I think that it's also talking about the positive consequences of our paying attention to the details of this story. I think this is—on one level—what the Talmud means when it says that the story was given "so that we may study it and reap reward."

If we study this story carefully, we will be able to identify and "remove the evil" from our midst. I don't mean this in an ominous, foreboding way. To the contrary, I think it's a wonderful thing to be able to gain clarity from a hypothetical case instead of real people having to endure actual misery. And so I hope that the study of these verses will help shed light on the dilemma of the addicted family and maybe help some people find the recovery that they need: this is my prayer.

Learning Early

They say that it is a wise person who can learn from someone else's mistakes. In the early days of AA, the only people who were working the Steps were low-bottom cases. As the decades went on, however, more and more people were coming into recovery *before* things had already gotten as bad as they can get.

The stark fact about addiction is that it is fatal. Whenever there is addiction, someone is eventually going to die before their natural time. So, whoever can get themselves into recovery before death is actually looming has already saved themselves quite a bit of misery.

The problem is that in order for recovery to work, it seems that the person must feel that things cannot possibly become worse than they are and still go on living. This is called "hitting bottom"—when there is just no deeper you can get.

Theoretically, a very wise person could read the story of the stubborn and rebellious son, identify with certain aspects of the story, and seek a solution to the problem before it has really developed into much at all. That would be ideal. That is the whole idea of "raising the bottom"—the attempt to show addicts the inevitability and predictability of their patterns *before* they actually have to go through every awful eventuality they have in store.

Practically, however, experience has shown repeatedly that until a person truly feels that they are on a path that is doomed, they will not begin to recover. Thus, for most addicts, the paradox of recovery is that things have to get a lot worse before they can start to get a little better.

Again, I pray that this book may play a part in helping someone come to a realization that will spare him or her even one extra moment of suffering. That is not in my control. I can only share what I know and leave it up to the reader to see whether he or she relates to what's being said here.

I honestly think that all of us human beings are addicts and we are all codependents, but that the severity and stage of our conditions exist on a wide spectrum. Some of us are naturally more adept at handling life than others, but all of us would benefit from working a program of recovery. It just seems that it's only the people whose lives have become a living hell who are willing to do the work.

In the following chapter, which begins the final section of this book, we will look at the idea of hitting bottom and why the admission of unmanageability is foundational to recovery.

PART VI
SURRENDER

Losing to win; accepting things as they are in order to change; saying you're sick in order to get well. Some of the major paradoxes of recovery.

CHAPTER 17
HITTING BOTTOM

Starting from Scratch

The idea of surrender presented in the First Step—"admitted we were *powerless* . . . that our lives had become *unmanageable*"—seems to turn many people off from even giving recovery an honest go. Yet, that's probably just as well, because the admission of powerlessness and unmanageability is not an *aspect* of recovery—it's the very *basis* of it. Nothing else seems to work very well without complete and unconditional capitulation first.

Hence, we find that before they can get better, most addicts need to get worse; they need to hit bottom.

Now, it's extremely important to qualify that bottom is *not* an objective term; to the contrary, it's very subjective. There are no rules for how bad your life has to be or how crazy you need to have become before you are allowed to say that you've had all you can take. When to call it quits is a judgment call that differs for everyone. Indeed, there are probably as many different bottoms in addiction as there are recovering addicts. In other words, you don't have to hit *the* bottom, just *your* bottom—whatever that means to you. Each of us has our own breaking point.

Whenever I speak to an active addict who has asked me for help and I want to see whether he or she is really ready for recovery, I usually ask, "Is this as bad as you ever want to feel again in your life?"

I also might ask, "Can you imagine things getting any more chaotic and not losing your mind?" or "Are you no longer willing to continue losing things that you used to think you would not allow yourself to lose?"

Only the individual can decide when he or she is sick and tired of being sick and tired. As many old-timers are wont to say, "When do you hit bottom? Whenever you stop digging."

You can't tell someone else that they've hit bottom. For codependents, this is particularly difficult to bear because while the addict may still be willing to go through more hell before he or she is ready to admit what's happening, the codependent may already be at the brink. Indeed, it's more common than not that in a marriage between a codependent and an addict, the codependent will hit bottom in their codependency before the addict has hit bottom in their addiction. If this is the case, the codependent can begin to recover even if the addict is still "doing more research," as we euphemistically put it.

At any rate, bottom is, just as we have said, a personal evaluation that only the individual can make. Some people can trudge on for years through the worst kinds of misery. Others hear their wake-up call earlier on. As the joke goes—"Bottom is the point at which your life is falling apart faster than you can lower your standards."

Raising the Bottom

As opposed to the early days when most people in recovery were actually walking in from skid row, most folks in recovery today are not "low-bottom" cases. Whether the addict is just starting to face consequences or already has one foot in the grave, it's all the same disease, and it follows the same inevitable pattern. You can cop to it at any point along the continuum. I once met a "high-bottom" drunk in AA who told me, "I'd rather spend the rest of my life in recovery trying to prove that I belong there than spend the rest of my life out of recovery trying to prove that I don't."

What Twelve-Step groups have done for many addicts is to effectively "raise the bottom" of addiction. Instead of playing things out to the end of death, insanity, or institutions, addicts can learn from the stories of others who followed the disease further down the hole and lived to tell the tale. This, incidentally, reminds me of another recovery saying—"What are the directions to recovery? Go to hell and make a U-turn."

Returning to God

In other words, you don't *have* to be on your very last leg to call out to God. You can turn things over to Him at any point you want. The problem is, it seems to be human nature that we cannot seem to bring ourselves to believe just how dependent we are and just how powerful He is until we are brought to the brink of utter collapse. But it doesn't *need* to be that way.

One of the innovative teachings of the Ba'al Shem Tov, was that even a *tzaddik*, a perfectly righteous individual, can "do" *teshuvah*. Usually translated as "repentance," *teshuvah* literally means "return"—returning to the intrinsic state of Oneness that is interrupted by ego-consciousness; in other words, recovery.

In the Ba'al Shem Tov's day, people thought of returning to God as the burden of penitents, those who had strayed from the path and were thus in need of rectification. That's why it was considered radical in his time when the Ba'al Shem Tov taught that one doesn't have to be guilty of anything to want to return to God. Sin is only the most blatant and egregious example of separation from God. The mere fact that one experiences life as a sentient being is something for which one can already do *teshuvah*— not as a form of penitence, but as a form of literally *restoring* the essential state of Oneness.

In other words, you can surrender to the One when your own existence becomes too crazy and painful to bear, which is surrender out of fear, or you can surrender to God now, out of love. The former is called humiliation; the latter is called humility. They both get you to the same place; one just necessitates going through more discomfort than the other.

Admission

One reason that people can take so long to surrender is that there's a terrible misunderstanding that surrender is the same as loss. But surrender is not loss. It's not even compromise. When you surrender you don't give up—anything. You just admit the truth; you give in to it. That's one of the reasons—just as the Ba'al Shem Tov taught—that even the perfectly righteous surrender to God. They want to live in harmony with truth. Surrender is not just for people who have mismanaged their lives. Surrender is the basis of relating to reality.

It's interesting that Judaism has a sort of First Step too, and it's about admission and surrender. It's not actually called the "First Step" but it is the first thing we're supposed to do each day.

Every morning when we rise, we humbly acknowledge our dependence upon God. This admission then serves as the foundation of everything else that we set out to do during the day. We cannot start building until we have that foundation:

Modeh ani li-fanecha, Melech Chai ve-Kayyam, she-hechezarta bi nish-masi be-chemlah; rabbah emunasecha.

I hereby acknowledge before You, Living and Eternal King, that You have most graciously restored my soul to me. Great is Your trustworthiness.

The first word of the prayer, *modeh*, is a verb that is often translated as "I thank." It does come from the same root word as *todah*, which is the noun for "thanks" or "gratitude," but it means much more than that. More accurately, *modeh* means "I acknowledge" or "I admit." I admit that I did not put myself here; I did not create my own life; I am not an existence apart from God but an extension of Him, very much dependent upon Him in every way and at all times. *Because* I admit this, I am *therefore* grateful.

In other words, the point is not so much to be thankful as to be honest, to acknowledge the truth. If one is in touch with reality, then one will *automatically* come to feel gratitude. Isn't it so that ingratitude is the rejection of reality while gratitude means to embrace it?

I don't think it would be overreaching to say that this feeling of simple and humble acceptance is *the most basic quality* of the Jewish people and of Judaism. The Hebrew word for Jew (*Yehudi*) does not just mean one who comes from Judah, but also "one who is *modeh*"—one who acknowledges, witnesses, praises, and hence "who is grateful." Everything else one does as a Jew is built upon the foundation of the simple acknowledgement that God is God and we are His people. It is from this acceptance and admission that all growth ensues and all healing takes place. We cannot begin our journey, in life or in each day, until we have first submitted to truth.

Total Immersion

In Hebrew, this state of humble recognition of our dependence on God is referred to as *bittul*, which literally means "nullification." Something that is in a state of *bittul*—something that is nullified—has lost its own identity by being included in something much greater. For instance, in terms of kosher dietary laws, if a single drop of milk were to fall into a large meat dish, although mixtures of milk and meat are prohibited, the negligible amount of milk is considered to have been *nullified* and does not render the meat dish forbidden. Indeed, the drop is disregarded and considered no longer even to exist. This is a physical illustration of the concept of *bittul*. Jewish mysticism uses the same word to describe abnegation of the ego.

The idea of self-surrender is evident in the kabbalistic custom of completely immersing oneself in a *mikveh*—a special ritual bath. The *mikveh* is a pool of water constructed for the purpose of spiritual purification. One who has contracted some form of ritual defilement removes the impurity by immersing in the *mikveh*.

Now, according to the Law, one who purifies in a *mikveh* must undergo *total* immersion. If even one body part is sticking out of the water, the immersion is invalid. One explanation is that through total immersion, one is returned, as it were, to the fetal state—floating in water, surrounded on all sides, unable to even draw a breath. In this state, one becomes acutely aware of one's utter dependence on God, like the fetus in the womb that is completely and utterly dependent and has no life separate from its mother. This realization is the epitome of humble acknowledgment and surrender. In this state of selflessness, in a state where one can hold on to nothing, one is reborn and, hence, purified. Everything else falls away; the slate is wiped clean.

It has been pointed out that the word for immersion (*tevilah*) is composed of the exact same letters in Hebrew as the word *habitul* (the self-nullification.)

Immersion	Self-Nullification
טבילה	הביטל

The Flood

It is significant that the minimum volume of a *mikveh* is set at forty units of a biblical measure called a *se'ah* (in total, about 200 gallons). These forty units are deemed the amount of water necessary to entirely envelop the average-sized human body. Chasidic commentaries draw a parallel between these forty units of water and the forty-day Flood that God brought upon the world in the time of Noah.

It's interesting because, viewed in this light, the Great Flood was not so much a punishment as a purification, a giant *mikveh* for the entire world, so to speak. Humanity hit bottom, was cleansed, and began anew.

The Chasidic masters teach that we should view personal crises in the same way. Whenever our challenges are so overwhelming as to bring us to our knees, we should not feel as if we are being punished, but that we are being purified. That does *not* mean that we are being purified *through* suffering. It does not mean that at all. It means that we are *released* from suffering by being *brought* to the point of surrender. There is a tremendous difference.

As soon as we can admit just how completely dependent we are upon God, the sooner the deluge will have served its real purpose and can be finished. One who immerses in a *mikveh* becomes purified in an instant, provided the immersion—the surrender—is total.

Surrender only takes an instant. And it doesn't even need to be the result of a major crisis. When we marvel at the miracle of being alive and drawing breath, when we are struck with awe and say, "I am alive, yet I did not give myself life. I exist, but I did not give myself existence"—that is humility. That is purification.

One of the reasons that old-timers still regularly attend meetings even after many years of sustained sobriety is so that they can associate with newcomers and be reminded of what early recovery is like. I have seen men and women with decades of recovery sit and quietly listen at a First Step Meeting while a bunch of people who may only have a few days of sobriety do all the talking. While there are no atheists in foxholes, there are plenty of people who stop praying after they've returned home from the battlefield.

Bottom line, it's easy to surrender when we're going through some terrible crisis. Maturity is the ability to admit our limitations and reliance on God beforehand, when things are still going well. In other words, hitting bottom is not what *makes* us powerless; it's what *convinces* us just how powerless we've really been all along.

Continuous Surrender

Many addicts will tell you that "The First Step is the only Step that I've gotta get perfect every day." You may be able to fudge on this or that aspect of your recovery and get away with it for a while, but the First Step—the admission of powerlessness and unmanageability—has to be there at all times.

Surrender is the very foundation of recovery, so the minute one "takes back" that Step, one also loses the whole structure that's built upon it.

Think about it. As we explained at length earlier in this book, the root of the problem is essentially a profound discomfort with existence that can only be relieved by allowing that existence to be in sync with its true state of oneness with God. Now, the ego is that which separates us or makes us feel separate from this oneness. This being the case, the only real obstacle to recovery is the ego and the path to recovery is the nullification of the same. All the rest of the Steps facilitate and maintain the self-abnegation that is begun in Step One. But without the initial and *ongoing* admission of powerlessness (at least powerlessness over one's addiction), the ego is still asserting control, still trying to take care of itself in a way that only God can do and the power struggle with reality continues.

In other words, the ego cannot make itself feel better about being an ego. Ego is the problem, not the solution. And by ego, we do not mean, arrogance or false pride. When we say ego, we mean just as we have already explained, the consciousness of self. The beginning of recovery is to give up our reliance on ego and realize that—as some in recovery have bluntly put it—"There is a God, and you are not Him."

Incidentally, that's what's so misguided, cruel, and counterproductive about the advice that many people give addicts—"Get a hold of yourself. Get some self-control. You could stop if you wanted." The addict's problem is not a *lack* of control but an obsession with it.

An alcoholic once explained to me, "Normal people drink so that they can *lose* control. I drink in order to *gain* control. When life makes me feel a certain way that I don't want to feel, I do the one thing that I know that I can count on to control how I feel."

It's true. "Normal" people may get drunk or high in order to cut loose and get away from their routine. Addicts get wasted so they can *face* their routine—whether it's work, family life, recreation, or any activity at all. A nonaddict may leave work early in order to go out and party, but only an addict parties early in order to go to work.

The more the addict feels frustration with other people and his or her environment, the more the compulsion there is to exert control over his or her own perceptions and feelings by self-medicating. That is why continuous surrender is necessary. Surrender isn't just the admission of having a problem that gets you into recovery; it's an ongoing state of mind that keeps you recovering for a lifetime.

If you've ever been to a Twelve-Step meeting and listened to what the people had to say, very little of it has to do with the struggle to maintain chemical abstinence. Most of what is talked about is the struggle to—as they say—"live life on life's terms."

One of my favorite recovery stories is something I heard secondhand from a woman in Al-Anon. At one meeting, she observed a woman who was clearly a newcomer trying to figure out what to do. Just before the meeting started, the newbie spotted another woman who was sitting at the front of the room and, assuming that this must be the group's leader, approached her for some direction.

"Are you in charge?" she asked.

"Oh, no," laughed the lady in front, slightly taken aback, "That's why I'm here. I'm trying *not* to be in charge!"

Pharaoh, Ego, and Unmanageability

In the Torah, the quintessential loser in life is Pharaoh, king of Egypt. Pharaoh had it all and lost everything, all because he couldn't admit powerlessness and unmanageability. He just couldn't surrender.

Pharaoh's persona illustrates how the opposite of good is not evil but selfishness. Evil is really just the way that selfishness expresses itself once it has given itself permission to do so. After all, who was Pharaoh—a tyrant, a murderer, an oppressor? All of these were but various manifestations of Pharaoh—particular character defects, if you will. But the essence of Pharaoh—that which made all of these other behaviors possible—was nothing more or less than self-worship, as Pharaoh so outrageously exclaimed, "I created myself." (Ezekiel 29:9).

The Zohar states that when God summoned Moses to confront Pharaoh in his palace, He did not say, "*Go* to Pharaoh," but rather "*Come* to Pharaoh," (Exodus 10:1), as if to say that He, God, was already there, and that by approaching Pharaoh, Moses was actually approaching God. How are we to understand this?

The Chasidic masters explain that God was revealing to Moses the secret of Pharaoh's power and the power of all evil—that, in essence, it is nothing more than the misappropriation of the power of God. In other words, the source of evil is the sense of independent, autonomous existence. It is not the outright rejection of God but the audacious delusion that God's power is one's own—in plain Yiddish, *chutzpah*.

Thus, God told Moses "Come to Pharaoh," as if to say, "Come, enter the essence of evil, and confront it at its source, as it really is. You will find that I am there already, for I am the Power that evil claims as its own."

In the end, Pharaoh's megalomania would be his own undoing. He would not allow himself to surrender to God until ten plagues had already devastated his nation. You would think that after the first few plagues, any normal person would have felt humbled. Blood, lice, frogs—that's all pretty unmanageable. But surrender was not part of Pharaoh's vocabulary. Even after finally releasing the slaves following the Death of the Firstborn, he quickly changed his mind and went chasing after them causing his legions to perish at the Splitting of the Sea. That is the essence of Pharaoh, the self-worshiping ego that will endure any abuse, any loss, as long as it does not have to surrender control.

The internal Pharaoh that is the root of addiction may be called by various names, such as will power or intelligence, but his message is always the same. He insists that he has things under control. By the time we realize that this Pharaoh's claims are untrue and that he is leading us into obliteration, his dominion over us is already complete. We stand face to face with evil, and it seems that there is nothing that we can do.

But then God beckons us, "Come. Come face the obsession as it really is. The ego is not the Power it claims to be, but to the contrary, it is absolute powerlessness."

Once we make this admission, it is then, and only then, that we can experience true power, the Power of God in our lives.

A Whole New You

Recovery is a process of giving up on old ideas—not just ideas about the world, but perhaps even more important, about oneself. The miraculous personal transformation that is effected by recovery is actually the result of a courageous surrender of self-concept, a willingness to be the person that God intended us to be.

We can learn much about this process by looking at the story of Abraham and his personal journey. At the age of seventy-five, Abraham received his first command from God, when he was ordered to leave his home and travel to the land that would eventually be given to him and his descendants. "Go out from your land, from your birthplace, and from your father's house, to the land which I will show you" (Genesis 12:1).

On a deeper level, God's command to Abraham to relocate is also an instruction to abandon every aspect of self and become something new and totally unknown to him.

Let's look at the wording of the verse again, this time explaining it according to its mystical interpretation.

"Go out from your land . . ."—The Hebrew word for "land," *eretz*, shares a common root with the word for "will," *ratzon*. God told Abraham to surrender his own desires and leave self-will behind.

". . . from your birthplace . . ."—God also told Abraham to abandon all of the traits that were a product of his environment and conditioning—all of the effects of his "birthplace."

". . . from your father's house . . ."—In Kabbalah, the capacity to generate new ideas is called "father," because the potential for insight is the progenitor of feelings and behavior. This means that God told Abraham to leave his intellectual preconditioning behind and allow himself to grasp an entirely new way of thinking.

". . . to the land which I will show you . . ."—God did not reveal to Abraham where he was heading, but only told him to leave where he was. He would be shown where to settle when he got there. This, in itself, is a great act of surrender.

The recovery from addiction is no less than the discovery of a new self that comes as a result of being ready to let go of everything one thinks is essential to his or her identity. As in the story of Abraham's journey, those who embark on the path of recovery start off having no idea where they are going or what they will become. Forsaking all that is known and comfortable, they simply surrender to God and trust that He is in charge.

The culmination of this process of self-surrender is actually true self-discovery mirroring the destination described in the journey of Abraham. "To the land which I will show you" may also be read as "to the land where I will show *you*." It is not that God just shows us the land; if we only let Him, God takes us to the place where He can show us who we really are.

Literal reading of Genesis 12:1	Deeper interpretation
Go out from your	Surrender of aspects of self
Land	Will
Birthplace	Conditioning
Father's house	Intellect
To the land which I will show you	Discovery of true self

The Nothing in Between

The Chasidic masters use a metaphor to explain why a something has to lose its old identity and become a nothing before it can become something new. A seed is a something. What is it? It's a seed. If you put it in the ground and tend to it, it will become something else—a tree. But in between being a perfectly good seed and becoming a tree, the seed has to fall apart. The seed actually starts to decompose in the ground, so that at one point, just before it starts to sprout, there is nothing. The seed is ruined and the new tree has yet to grow.

On a similar note, the kabbalists tell us that when souls in Paradise ascend from one level to the next, they must first undergo another "cleansing"—an erasing of their memory—similar to that which occurs when the soul first transitions out of physical embodiment and into the spiritual world. The reason for this is the same as the principle illustrated by the metaphor of the seed. In order to change a little, one can build on what one has already become, but in order to change drastically, one has to completely let go of what one was.

In this sense, hitting bottom and surrendering is like rebirth. As I heard it nicely put, "When you're down to nothing, God's up to something." We can't make miracles happen; but we can certainly allow them to happen through us—*if* we are humble enough to get out of the way. Surrender—especially daily surrender when life seems perfectly fine and manageable—is how we keep ourselves clear and open so that we may channel God's power in our lives.

The Power of Powerlessness

God gave the Torah at Mount Sinai. The Chasidic masters have observed that the two words—"mount" and "Sinai"—that make up the name of the place of unparalleled Godly revelation are actually opposites.

A mountain represents grandeur and stature. The word Sinai is rooted in the Hebrew word *seneh*, a thornbush, which symbolizes lowliness and an unassuming nature. The combination of the two words into the single name "Mount Sinai" indicates a melding of both characteristics—boldness and humility together.

The Lubavitcher Rebbe explained that regarding our spiritual development, the three terms—Mountain, Sinai, and Mount Sinai—represent three progressive phases in our growth.

The first level is that of Sinai—abject humility. At the beginning of our spiritual development, we must necessarily embrace our own nothingness. Any feeling of pride at this point is out of place. This is precisely what is meant by surrender or hitting bottom.

As we progress, we come to the level called Mount Sinai—a combination of the two words. At this stage, we have sufficiently reduced the ego so that we may actually begin to experience feelings of power that do not come from self-reliance but rather from a sense of being reliant upon the strength of God. At the same time, however, the mountain must be balanced by Sinai, for we have not yet come to such a degree of surrender where any sense of power that we feel is certain to be emanating solely from the power of God.

Finally, the single word "mountain" embodies the ultimate level of spiritual development. This state is achieved when we are so entirely nullified before God that it is not even necessary to mention the humility of Sinai. Our sense of personal surrender is so pervasive that it is obvious that any strength we may feel comes only from our total reliance upon God's strength and not our own.

Many critics of recovery argue that the program's insistence that one must surrender to a Higher Power is demeaning to addicts. To this charge, I would only reply that people who are ready for recovery don't need a program to help them feel bad about themselves. The consequences of active addiction do a fine job of that already. However, and more important, what these critics fail to understand is that by admitting our own powerlessness—and thereby coming to rely upon God—we find an inner strength that willful self-reliance could never deliver. This is the paradox of all growth—that through surrender we become strong, and that by facing our own lack of power we come to know and feel what real Power is.

CHAPTER 18
ACCEPTANCE

Two Plus Two Is Four

When I was a teenager, my father, who is a psychologist, asked me, "Do you know the difference between a psychotic and a neurotic?" I said that I didn't. "A psychotic," he proceeded to explain, "is someone who thinks that two plus two equals five. A neurotic knows that two plus two equals four . . . *and can't stand it*!"

Little did I realize at the time that my father had transmitted to me an important spiritual principle. What psychologists call *neurosis*, and philosophers might call *hubris*, the folks in recovery call *playing God*. Whether we look through the lenses of psychology, religion, philosophy, or recovery, there seems to be general agreement to at least one aspect of human happiness and health. Certain things are what they are. Fighting them, as such, is altogether unproductive, arrogant, silly, and even tragic—like Don Quixote tilting at windmills. Well-adjusted people just don't declare war against the fact that two plus two is four.

In recovery, major emphasis is placed on practicing "acceptance." Acceptance almost sounds like a highfalutin clinical term, but it really just means to relax and get over the fact that things may not always be just as you want them to be—and that's fine. Another big word in recovery is *serenity*, which means pretty much the same thing.

Worry, anxiety, anger, dread—these are all highly unspiritual qualities. We're supposed to stay above the fray and be calm and tranquil.

On the other hand, the human being uniquely possesses free choice to make decisions and take actions. God gave us the ability not just to accept the status quo but also to make positive change.

So which is it? Which is the more desirable trait? Taking decisive action, or accepting "facts" as they are?

Of course, the answer is both. Or, more accurately, it depends.

It depends on what we're dealing with. Some things call for acceptance, and others things call for action.

Which leaves us with the $64,000 Question.

How do we know which things to accept and which things to change?

The Serenity Prayer

Perhaps the most famous words associated with recovery are the words of Serenity Prayer. In just a few brief lines, the prayer encapsulates the great conundrum of which we speak:

God, grant me the serenity to accept the things I cannot change, the courage to change the things I can, and the wisdom to know the difference.

I'm going to go on a sort of tangent for a moment, but since it's something that I am asked about so often, I would like to talk about the origins of the Serenity Prayer. In my experience, it is very common for Jewish people in recovery to wonder whether it's ideal or even okay for them to say this prayer. So, let's put our discussion of the prayer's content on hold for a bit and talk about its history.

For the record, the Serenity Prayer was first used in connection with recovery in 1942, when the staff at AA headquarters in New York saw it included, without attribution, in a newspaper obituary. "Never had we seen so much AA in so few words," cofounder Bill Wilson would later write.

To this day, there are still many theories about the prayer's true authorship. As Wilson also wrote, "No one can tell for sure who first wrote the Serenity Prayer. Some say it came from the early Greeks; others think it was from the pen of an anonymous English poet; still others claim it was written by an American Naval officer. . . ."

It is generally accepted that the prayer was composed—at least in its current and most famous version—by the American theologian Reinhold Niebuhr, who is said to have written the prayer for a sermon he gave in the 1930s, though Niebuhr himself admitted that he could never be certain whether or not he unconsciously adapted the prayer from some other source. "It may have been spooking around for years, even centuries," Niebuhr told AA's magazine, *The Grapevine*, in 1950.

At any rate, what is germane to our discussion is that the prayer is not known to appear anywhere in any denomination's liturgy. It seems that it is just an old idea that has been passed around in different forms throughout the years, and that Niebuhr, who was a Christian, is the one who drafted—or at least made famous—the version that is popular today. In that sense, I can't see much of a difference between a Jew's reciting the Serenity Prayer and reading the words "In God we trust" on an American dollar bill.

Now, let's return to our main discussion. We were faced with a question: What needs to be accepted, and what needs to be changed?

The Serenity Prayer doesn't seem to give us an answer; it just confirms that there is a legitimate question.

Now an easy (but all together unsatisfying) answer would be to say that this is precisely *why* the Serenity Prayer is a *prayer*. Since we have no way of knowing what must be accepted and what must be changed, we ask God to give us wisdom and let us know. But as I said, that answer doesn't do it for me.

I think that there are some general guidelines that we can learn that can help us to know when we need the serenity to accept things and when we need the courage to make a change. I also think that it is lack of understanding about this distinction that gives rise to the frequently hysterical disapproval of how acceptance and serenity are practiced in recovery.

Everything Is in the Hands of Heaven

The Jewish view on this matter is clear. The Talmud says, "Everything is in the hands of Heaven except for one's awe of Heaven."

It is an unequivocal statement. It's black and white. God controls reality, every bit of it. We control our attitude, every bit of it. In other words, everything that *happens* to us is up to God, but the way we *feel* about it is up to us.

In this light, it is clear that "the things we cannot change" means every aspect of objective reality while that which we must have the courage to change is just one thing—how we view the reality. In other words, all we can change is our opinion about God and the job that He is doing running the world, but we cannot run the world.

It is worthwhile to note that the sages employed the term *"awe* of Heaven" to describe the perceptions we choose. Why specifically awe? Why not, say, love?

Because awe is the other side of the same coin as courage. The more we fear God, the less we fear things that are finite and fleeting, and hence, the more equipped we are to handle life as it comes. If we are in awe of God, then we are not overwhelmed by the world.

When he was five years old, the Ba'al Shem Tov became an orphan. Just before his father passed, he told his son, "Yisrolik [the diminutive of the Ba'al Shem Tov's given name], fear nothing but God alone." This is a deep concept. There is a lot of meaning hidden in these words.

As we have noted in an earlier chapter, Judaism believes in a God who is all-powerful and always in control. Knowing that one's life is entirely in God's hands should logically inspire one to feel the utmost reverence of Him. Equally important is the corollary to the awe of Heaven—a *lack of awe* of things that we can't control anyway.

If one believes that God is in absolute control, then one will not erroneously attribute power to any other beings. In other words, the Ba'al Shem Tov's father gave him the formula for serenity and courage. "Fear nothing." How? By fearing "God alone."

The eleventh-century Jewish philosopher Rabbi Bachya ibn Pakuda expressed the same concept quite succinctly in his classic *Duties of the Heart*:

> When a person feels that no created entity has the ability to help him or harm him without the permission of the Creator, then his heart will turn away from fear of them or hope in these things and will trust in the Creator alone.

In other words, the more one acknowledges that God's power is absolute, the more one is relieved of emotional dependence upon all kinds of transitory conditions. One who relies only on God will never be afraid of any fact of his or her own life. Awe of heaven is the flipside of and corollary to serenity, contentment, and freedom.

To once again quote Ibn Pakuda:

> He will be happy with whatever God brings him. . . . He will not desire anything that God has not chosen for him and will want only what God wants for him . . . . In worldly matters, he will not prefer one condition over another nor desire to be in any other condition than the one he is in.

Material vs. Spiritual

Another way of viewing this same formula is by classifying all matters as either material or spiritual. The "everything" that is "in the hands of Heaven" refers to the material conditions of our lives, while the "except for the awe of Heaven," which is in *our* hands, refers to our spiritual state over which we have been granted free will. In other words, I don't have power over the conditions God puts me in, but I do have the power to make moral decisions regardless of those conditions. As the Talmud says, already from the time that a child is conceived, it is decreed from Heaven whether that child will be "strong or weak, wise or foolish, rich or poor. And yet," says the Talmud, "righteous or wicked is *not* decreed, for ... 'All is in the hands of Heaven except for one's awe of Heaven.' "

There's an old Chasidic expression, "The goat's job is to give milk. The goatherd's job is to take care of her." What this means is that we "goats" only have to do one thing; we have to fulfill the mission that God has given us. The "Goatherd" takes care of the rest. And just like a goat doesn't worry about the goatherd's responsibilities, neither should we waste our time figuring out how God should run the world. As I heard one recovering addict put it nicely, "I try to do God's work; *not* God's job." When we stay focused on *our* duties—our spirituality—and stay out of God's business—our physicality—things seem to work out best.

A story is told about a young and gifted Torah scholar who met with the first Chabad Rebbe, Rabbi Schneur Zalman, in a private audience. The Rebbe told him, "Spirituality and physicality are essentially opposites. A superior quality of the physical is a deficiency of the spiritual. In material matters, being happy with one's lot is the greatest of virtues. But in spiritual matters, being happy with one's lot is the worst deficiency there can be."

In light of what we have already explained, this makes perfect sense. Since material matters are really out of our hands, then it makes no sense to lament over what we think we are lacking in that area. To the contrary, because God is in control and will always give us what's best for us, then the healthiest and most rational disposition to have regarding these things is contentment and gratitude. But when it comes to our spiritual condition, what kind of person we are, and how hard we are working on our growth, we have no reason to ever be satisfied. There is always something more that we can do. Indeed, it is truly the *only* thing we can do.

People, Places, and Things

To one who is not in recovery, "people, places, and things" sounds like an English grammar lesson on nouns, but to Twelve-Steppers, the reference is an immediately recognizable spiritual axiom. "People, places, and things" is essentially recovery-speak for "All is in the hands of Heaven except for one's awe of Heaven." What am I powerless over? People, places, and things. What is in God's hands? People, places, and things. What do I have to stop being stressed out about and trying to control? People, places, and things.

The exact origin of this now ubiquitous turn of phrase is unknown, at least to me, but a similar expression is used in a personal story entitled "Acceptance Was the Answer" in later editions of the Big Book:

> When I am disturbed, it is because I find some person, place, thing or situation—some fact of my life—unacceptable to me, and I can find no serenity until I accept that person, place, thing or situation as being exactly the way it is supposed to be at this moment. Nothing, absolutely nothing happens in God's world by mistake. Until I could accept my alcoholism, I could not stay sober; unless I accept life completely on life's terms, I cannot be happy. I need to concentrate not so much on what needs to be changed in the world as on what needs to be changed in me and in my attitudes. (p. 417)

A Final Word on Faith

It's unfortunate that so many people misunderstand the idea of acceptance and confuse it with timidity or meekness when that is so much the opposite of the truth. Any recovering addict can tell you that the self-reliance of active addiction is a life of terror, but the God-reliance of recovery is a life of courage.

Another assumption is that acceptance makes us passive. The irony is that it is a *lack* of acceptance that paralyzes us in our lives and cuts us off from growth. I think it may safely be said that even from a very rational and clinical standpoint, the less energy we expend on things that are not our business, the more energy we have to live our lives contentedly and effectively. And although one can debate whether there is an underlying spiritual truth that governs the distinction between the two, for most addicts in recovery, it seems to work best to accept that we're talking plain and simple about relying on God.

There are many reasons that we may be prejudiced against faith. Perhaps we have been jaded by experiences, or maybe we suffer from intellectual pride. But the proof, as they say, is in the pudding. The power and the strength drawn from "letting go and letting God" can be seen in every miraculous story of personal recovery. Reliance on God is not a liability but the greatest possible asset. As a former self-avowed agnostic in the program once told me, "At first I thought the God thing was a crutch. Turns out that it's stilts."

As we wrap up this small chapter on a very large concept, I'd like to quote an excerpt from the Big Book that I am moved to include here not only for the relevance of its subject but also for the beauty of its prose:

> We trust infinite God rather than our finite selves. We are in the world to play the role He assigns. Just to the extent that we do as we think He would have us, and humbly rely on Him, does He enable us to match calamity with serenity.
>
> We never apologize to anyone for depending upon our Creator. We can laugh at those who think spirituality the way of weakness. Paradoxically, it is the way of strength. The verdict of the ages is that faith means courage. All men of faith have courage. They trust their God. We never apologize for God. Instead we let Him demonstrate, through us, what He can do. (p. 68)

Do We Ever Get Well?

Is it really true that "once an addict, always an addict"?

Another problem that many people have with recovery is that there is no such thing as being issued a clean bill of health. There's no graduation day, so to speak.

But how can people who've been sober for years—decades even—still go to meetings regularly and, moreover, identify themselves each and every time as alcoholics or addicts?

Personally, I don't have a hard time accepting that addiction can be treated but never cured. For me, the model for this already exists in Jewish teachings, particularly in Chasidic mysticism.

We have mentioned a few times in this book some of the teachings of the first Rebbe of Chabad, the great Chasidic master, Rabbi Schneur Zalman. I find it important to mention now that Rabbi Schneur Zalman, also known as the Alter Rebbe, wrote an entire book as a systematic guide for actualizing personal potential. The book is called *Tanya*, and its premise is that anyone who earnestly applies the methods clearly outlined in the book can attain personal perfection and, with continued effort, consistently maintain that state for the rest of his or her life.

The definition of perfection, however, is not what most people might think.

The Alter Rebbe points out an interesting dichotomy in the human condition. On the one hand, we are fallible by nature, prone to selfishness and self-justification. On the other hand, we have been endowed with the ability to control our impulses. We are not animals. Perfection, as such, is not defined by being rid of one's ugly nature. Perfection means that one is vigilant never to allow these impulses to manifest as actual behaviors.

In other words, although we might not *be* perfect, we still have the choice to *do* perfect. *That* is the perfection that the Alter Rebbe tells us we can achieve—to become a person who despite being rife with imperfections on the inside, chooses to behave perfectly on the outside. It's not easy, but it is certainly within reach. As long as we do what we need to do, we can keep the inner beast in check. Conversely, if we let up, it will have dominion over us before we know it.

I believe that this concept can help us to understand the disease model of addiction. The Twelve Steps outline a program by which we can live a happy and productive life in spite of still suffering from addiction. The Steps don't get rid of the disease; they keep it in check. In clinical terms, this is what one might call "remission." In the words of the Big Book (p. 85), "What we really have is a daily reprieve contingent on the maintenance of our spiritual condition."

And so, to answer the question, "Do we ever get well?" Sure! Absolutely! With recovery, we can get very, very well. But in order to *stay* well, we have to continue doing the same things that helped us in the first place.

Jacob and Esau

In the Book of Genesis, there's a story about the matriarch Rebecca and her very difficult pregnancy. Not knowing that she is carrying twins, she asks God to tell her why she is in so much pain. She discovers not only that she is carrying two babies, but that they are actually battling within her. Her sons, Jacob and Esau, are rivals who are destined to continually struggle from inside the womb throughout their lives and into the annals of history. "And God said to her, 'Two nations are in your womb, and two peoples shall diverge from your belly; and one nation will struggle against the other' " (Genesis 25:23).

The fate of Jacob and Esau is such that they cannot both exert power at the same time. Each one's strength is derived only from the weakening of the other. As tradition relates, "They will never be equal. When one rises, the other will fall."

In spiritual terms, Jacob and Esau represent our two diametrically opposed inclinations within us—our desire to serve God and our desire to serve ourselves. Jacob represents spirituality, humility, and meekness, whereas Esau represents physicality, arrogance, and aggression. As the Chasidic masters teach, not only within Rebecca, but also in all of us, these two twins struggle, always vying for control of the other.

We may view the disease of addiction as having its own personality, the internal voice of selfishness and gratification. It wants to control our lives so that we pursue only its desires. Like Esau, it is the older twin—big and strong, a hunter and an outlaw. Then there is a part of us that wants to be closer to God and live a life of usefulness. This is the younger, softer brother, who is quiet, peaceful, and loving. These two "twins" cannot both be in charge at the same time; neither can they share nor divvy up control to coexist on equal footing. There is no possibility of compromise. Each one can only strengthen itself at the direct expense of the other.

Like the image of a seesaw, if one end is rising, then the other must be going down. At any given moment, the addict inside may push itself up over our spiritual self; or, conversely, our spirituality comes to the fore through the quelling and repressing of our disease for another little while. But one thing is certain—both cannot happen at once.

As I heard one old-timer put it, "Ask yourself at this moment, 'Are you working on your recovery or on your relapse?' "

One Step Ahead

The aforementioned book of *Tanya* explains that even those who actually exert perfect control over their negative impulses retain their inner Esau. *Doing* perfect does not equate to *being* perfect. The potential for selfishness—even when kept in total check—never just goes away. To the contrary, it explains that just by our maintaining our bodily needs, our animalistic side unavoidably grows stronger every day.

It comes as no wonder, then, that the experts on addiction tell us that the disease not only remains dormant during sobriety, but also actually *progresses*. Many addicts have served as unfortunate examples of that fact. When the disease is allowed to gain the upper hand—even after many years—it doesn't just pick up where it left off. It catches up almost instantly to where it would be had the addict never recovered at all.

I once heard an addict with many years of continuous sobriety explain his personal take on the status of his disease. "Turn up a stereo to full blast and then unplug it and leave. Come back two, five, even ten years later, and if you plug it in again, the stereo will be instantly playing on full blast."

The only choice is to exert constant control. The disease will never compromise, nor will it just go away. It doesn't atrophy. It doesn't get tired of trying.

Thankfully, God has given each of us the ability to stay one step—or, let's hope, many steps—ahead. It is our relationship with God that is the key to outrunning, outlasting, and overpowering the negativity within us—one day at a time.

Those addicts who maintain long-term sobriety all know the secret that when it comes to spiritual growth, we need to renew our commitment daily with refreshed intensity and vigor. We must remain ever vigilant. We can settle for no less than a goal of complete domination of all aspects of our lives.

Does this sound extreme or intense? It is—because the disease is. And on this count, who can afford to be outdone?

Being and Doing

I have heard people in recovery explain, "We are sick people trying to get well, not bad people trying to be good."

This important distinction comforts many people. The problem that's left is that just as people don't want to think of themselves as bad, they don't want to think of themselves as sick either. I have heard many a relapsed addict tell me those very words. "It's not good for us to keep thinking of ourselves as sick." Of course, the irony is that the people who believe they're still sick are doing what they need to do to continue enjoying life sober, and the people who say they're all better are out there dying a miserable, slow (and sometimes not so slow) death.

To help better understand this concept, I think it's valuable to reiterate the aforementioned difference between *being* and *doing*.

When people introduce themselves at Twelve-Step meetings by saying, "My name is so-and-so, and I'm a fill-in-the-blank," they're not talking about what they *do* but who they *are*. The statement that "I *am* an addict" doesn't describe a behavior. There's no shame or blame in that.

See, we can be appropriately remorseful for our actions, but we really have no reason to ever be ashamed of who we are. It is our *choices* that define us, our *choices* for which we take responsibility, not our identities.

I happen to think that there's something very Jewish about that.

I remember when I was a kid and Jimmy Carter first ran for president. A journalist asked him if he had ever been unfaithful in his marriage, to which Carter's solemn response was, "I've looked on a lot of women with lust. I've committed adultery in my heart many times," to which he then added: "This is something that God recognizes, that I will do and have done, and God forgives me for it."

What is that supposed to mean? Was Carter admitting to having natural urges and desires? And, indeed, if that was the case, should we care? What kind of news is that?

Imagine asking a Jew, "Did you ever eat on Yom Kippur?" and he answers, "I felt hungry in my stomach."

You felt hungry. That's not a moral issue. It's a physiological issue. You were hungry. And even if you say that you felt hungry when it was only an hour into Yom Kippur and your stomach was still full from your prefast meal, then it is still just an emotional or psychological issue. The bottom line is that you did not eat! You didn't *do* it. You didn't *talk* about doing it. You didn't even entertain it as a serious *thought*. You *felt* it.

That's why Carter's statement about lusting in his heart makes little sense. If he was trying to convey that he had felt urges, then what substance is there to his "confession"? It seems rather like admitting to having driven fifty miles per hour in a school zone ... "in your heart."

If, on the other hand, what he was saying is that he hadn't just felt impulses but actually calculated and made plans to act them out and just never went through with them, then that might be worthy of mention. But then the tag-on about God recognizing this and forgiving him makes no sense. Why should God give out a free pass for a person's scheming just because the All-Knowing is aware of it before it happens?

Judaism, however, recognizes that if we're human, then we obviously suffer from the human condition. That's who we *are*. At the same time, the human condition is a poor excuse for misconduct. Whatever our foibles and flaws, behavior is a decision, and if we choose to do the wrong thing, we have no one to blame but ourselves—because that's what we *do*.

Addiction is no exception. On the one hand, addicts will always be addicts—even in recovery—and they identify as such at every meeting. But that's just who they *are*. What they *do* is work the Steps, enjoy life, and stay sober. And if they don't, well . . . relapse is also something one *does*; it's also a choice. Although nobody chooses to be an addict, an addict may choose to stop doing the things that addicts need to do to recover.

Progress, Not Perfection

From all of this, it may sound as if we're trying to convince you that recovering addicts are all superholy people who live flawlessly spiritual lives.

And the moment they don't—*WHAM!* Down for the count!

That would be incorrect.

When we talk about constantly staying a step ahead of the disease, we don't mean to imply that there is no room for mistakes or that even in recovery addicts don't do stupid, even rotten, things that they later regret.

It says in the Big Book:

> No one among us has been able to maintain anything like perfect adherence to these principles [The Twelve Steps]. We are not saints. The point is, that we are willing to grow along spiritual lines. The principles we have set down are guides to progress. We claim spiritual progress rather than spiritual perfection. (p. 60)

There's a good reason why many sponsors have their sponsees go through the Steps repeatedly, and it's not just to keep folks from getting bored. It's that most people do not do each and every Step correctly the first time. It's to be expected, and it's perfectly fine. Each of us can only do our best *for now*—and then keep growing.

On the other hand, there is one thing that the addict is supposed to get right each and every time, and that is to remain perfectly abstinent of their drug of choice.

I have heard people say that relapse is a part of recovery. That sounds very funny to me, to say the least. Granted, *after* the fact, a relapse can help someone to get serious and become more committed to recovery, but no one in their right mind is going out and relapsing in order to recover any more than people hit bottom the first time for the purpose of being eligible to join a recovery program.

There is no excuse for relapse, only an explanation. And that explanation is invariably that the addict stopped doing something that he or she needed to be doing—like working the Steps, talking to his or her sponsor, going to meetings, or working with others. The relapse didn't just *happen*.

Certainly, the admission of powerlessness made in the First Step is not an excuse either. To the contrary, powerlessness over one's addiction means that once one starts, then all bets are off. But whether or not to get started again is a *choice*. That's what they mean when they say that one drink is too many and a thousand is never enough.

The point is that being an addict doesn't mean that you have to loose your life to the disease of addiction. Thank God, in this day and age in which we live, there are choices.

Very few people, if any, are very happy when they finally realize that they're addicts. But those who are in recovery will tell you that it's the greatest news they ever found out about themselves.

No Accident

I'll just try to wrap things up here with a final thought.

There is a commandment in the Torah that by definition is impossible to set out to do intentionally.

What is it?

If you are out in the field reaping your harvest and forget a sheaf, you are forbidden, upon realizing the oversight, to go back and fetch it. It is a mitzvah for the forgotten sheaf to be left for the poor. Thus, by *not* going back and picking up the sheaf, you do a mitzvah.

Now, through the performance of any commandment, a degree of holiness is drawn down into this world, but the teachings of Chasidus explain that the commandment concerning the forgotten sheaf elicits a uniquely lofty energy from on High—so lofty, indeed, that we cannot deliberately access it. And this is precisely why the performance of this commandment can come about only after the fact, by accident.

In terms of our service of God, the commandment of the forgotten sheaf teaches us that there can be certain opportunities that are so sublime that they cannot be evoked through a deliberate act. They are so holy that we do not have the power to make them happen. They have to come along on their own, indeed, without our even knowing that that's what's happening. Only by forgetting the sheaf in the field can one fulfill the commandment of leaving it there. Only by realizing that one is an addict can one begin to recover.

It is unclear whether addicts are born that way or if they somehow cross some invisible point of no return at some stage of their using. What is certain, however, is that nobody sets out to become addicted so that they can later be deemed eligible for recovery.

Perhaps the reason that this is so is that, like the commandment of the forgotten sheaf, recovery draws down such a lofty degree of holiness that it is not something that anyone can purposely set out for. Its level of spirituality is something so rare that it can only be begrudgingly discovered, as if by accident.

Of course, there's really no such thing as accidents. No chance or coincidence either. It's just that, sometimes, God seems to think it's best to remain anonymous.

APPENDICES

Some Twelve-Step Groups

AlAnon/Alateen	For friends and family members of alcoholics
AA	Alcoholics Anonymous
CA	Cocaine Anonymous
CLA	Clutterers Anonymous
CMA	Crystal Meth Anonymous
CoAnon	For friends and family of addicts
CoDA	CoDependents Anonymous
COSA	Codependents of Sex Addicts
COSLAA	CoSex and Love Addicts Anonymous
DA	Debtors Anonymous
EA	Emotions Anonymous
EHA	Emotional Health Anonymous
FA	Families Anonymous
GA	Gamblers Anonymous
GamAnon/GamATeen	For friends and family members of problem gamblers
MA	Marijuana Anonymous
NA	Narcotics Anonymous
NAIL	Neurotics Anonymous
NarAnon	For friends and family members of addicts
NicA	Nicotine Anonymous
OA	Overeaters Anonymous
OLGA	Online Gamers Anonymous
SA	Sexaholics Anonymous
SA	Smokers Anonymous
SAA	Sex Addicts Anonymous
SCA	Sexual Compulsives Anonymous
SIA	Survivors of Incest Anonymous
SLAA	Sex and Love Addicts Anonymous
SocAA	Social Anxiety Anonymous
SPA	Social Phobics Anonymous
WA	Workaholics Anonymous

GLOSSARY OF RABBINIC SOURCES

Abba, Rabbi (2nd century CE): Mishnaic sage, student of R. Shimon bar Yochai; transcriber of The Zohar.

Akiva, Rabbi (R. Akiva ben Joseph) (c. 50-c.135 CE): Among the greatest of the Mishnaic sages; one of the Ten Martyrs.

Alter Rebbe: See R. Schneur Zalman of Liadi.

Baal Shem Tov, R. Israel (lit. "Master of the Good Name") (1698-1760): Rabbi Yisrael ben Eliezer, founder of Chasidus.

Bachya ben Joseph ibn Pakuda (1040-1080): Saragossa, Spain; author of Duties of the Heart; often referred to as Rabbeinu Bachya.

Chananya ben Tradyon (1st century CE): Mishnaic sage, one of the Ten Martyrs, See Rabbi Akiva and Rabbi Chanina Deputy High Priest.

Chanina Deputy High Priest (1st century CE): Mishnaic sage, one of the Ten Martyrs, See Rabbi Akiva and Chananya ben Tradyon.

Chasidus: The teachings of the Chasidic masters, starting from the Ba'al Shem Tov and continuing with his disciples.

Cordovero, Rabbi Moshe(1522-1570 CE): Known as "the Ramak," Kabbalist in Safed, Israel.

R. DovBer of Lubavitch (1773-1827): Second Chabad Rebbe, son and successor of the Alter Rebbe, and uncle and father-in-law of the Tzemach Tzedek.

Duties of the Heart: See Bachya ibn Pakuda.

Ha-Levi, Judah (c.1075–1141 C.E.): Spanish Jewish physician, poet and philosopher; considered one of the greatest Hebrew poets; author of the classic philosophical work The Kuzari.

Hillel (d. 9 CE): Mishnaic sage, native of Babylon, known for his statement, "What is hateful to you, do not do to your fellowman."

Hirsch, Rabbi Samson Raphael (1808-1888): Talmudist, scholar, philosopher, prolific author and Rabbi of Frankfurt am Main, Germany.

Kook, Rabbi Abraham Isaac (1865–1935): Assumed position of first Ashkenazic Chief Rabbi of the British Mandate in 1920.

Kotzk, The Rabbi of, R. Menachem Mendel Morgensztern (1787-1859): Austrian Galicia; chasidic master known for his profound aphorisms.

Kuzari: See Judah Ha-Levi.

Laws Concerning the Prohibition of Idolatry: See Maimonides.

Laws of the Foundations of the Torah: See Maimonides.

Lubavitcher Rebbe, The, R. Menachem Mendel Schneerson (1902-1994): Seventh leader of Chabad-Lubavitch; Known for his unique scholarship and radical, global activism for world Jewry.

Maimonides: Rabbi Moses ben Maimon (1135-1204): known by the acronym the "Rambam"; Cordoba (Spain), Fez (Morocco) and Fostat (old Cairo, Egypt); codifier, philosopher, communal leader.

Meir, Rabbi (2nd century CE): Mishnaic sage, husband of Berurya and son-in-law of Chananya ben Tradyon. Student of Rabbi Akiva.

Meiri, Rabbi Menachem (1249-c. 1310): Catalan rabbi, talmudist and Maimonides scholar.

R. Menachem Mendel of Lubavitch, (1789-1866): Known as the Tzemach Tzedek; Third leader of Chabad-Lubavitch; son-in-law and successor of R. Dovber of Lubavitch; grandson of R. Schneur Zalman of Liadi.

Midrash: Classical collection of the Sages' homiletic interpretations of the Torah.

Mishnah: Earliest written compilation of the orally transmitted teachings of the Torah, compiled c. 200 C.E.

Principles of Faith: See Maimonides

R. Schneur Zalman of Liadi (1745-1812): Founder and first Rebbe of the Chabad branch of chassidism; known also as the "Alter Rebbe;" author of Tanya.

Simeon ben Yohai, Rabbi (c. 100-160 CE): Mishnaic sage and mystic; student of Rabbi Akiva; Author of the Zohar.

Talmud: Basic compendium of Jewish law and thought; its tractates mainly comprise discussions elucidating the germinal statements of law collectively known as the Mishnah; edited in Babylonia, end of the fifth century C.E.

Tanya: See Schneur Zalman of Liadi.

Tzemach Tzedek: See R. Menachem Mendel of Lubavitch.

Zohar: Main text of the Kabbalah based on the teachings of Rabbi Shimon bar Yochai (c. 100-160 CE) See Shimon bar Yochai, see Rabbi Abba.

R. Zushya of Anipoli (1718?-1800): Chasidic master of the second generation from the Ba'al Shem Tov.; Anipoli (Hanipol) Ukraine.